IN SEARCH OF PREVENTION

In Search of Prevention

The MARS Project

ROGER FULLER
Social Work Research Centre
University of Stirling

Avebury

Aldershot · Brookfield USA · Hong Kong · Singapore · Sydney

Published by
Avebury
Ashgate Publishing Limited
Gower House
Croft Road
Aldershot
Hants GU11 3HR
England

Ashgate Publishing Company
Old Post Road
Brookfield
Vermont 05036
USA

A CIP catalogue record for this book is available from the British Library and the US Library of Congress.

ISBN 1 85628 349 6

Printed and Bound in Great Britain by
Athenaeum Press Ltd., Newcastle upon Tyne.

Contents

Series Editor's Preface

Evaluative Studies in Social Work brings together research which has explored the impact of social work services in a variety of contexts and from several perspectives. The vision of social work in this series is a broad one. It encompasses services in residential, fieldwork and community settings undertaken by workers with backgrounds in health and welfare. The volumes will therefore include studies of social work with families and children, with elderly people, people with mental and other health problems and with offenders.

This approach to social work is consistent with contemporary legislation in many countries, including Britain, in which social work has a key role in the assessment of need and in the delivery of personal social services, in health care and in criminal justice. It also continues a long tradition which perceives an integral relationship between social work, social research and social policy. Those who provide social work services are acquainted with the complexities of human need and with the achievements and shortcomings of major instruments of social policy. This knowledge was exploited by, amongst others, Booth, Rowntree and the Webbs in their studies of poverty. Politicians and sociologists have also recognised that, together with the people they try to help, social workers can provide a commentary on the human meaning of public policies and the social issues that grow from private troubles.

This knowledge and experience of the recipients and practitioners of social work is not, of course, immediately accessible to the wider community. A major purpose of research is to gather, organise and interpret this information and, in the studies in this series, to evaluate the impact of social work. Here there are many legitimate interests to consider. First and foremost are direct service users and those who care for them. These are the people who should be the main beneficiaries of social work services. Also to be considered are the personnel of other services for whom liaison and collaboration with social work is essential to their own successful functioning. The needs and views of these different groups may well conflict and it is the researcher's task to identify those tensions and describe social work's response to them.

The problems which confront social work are often extremely complex. They may need to be tackled in a variety of ways; for example, through practical assistance, advocacy, counselling and supervision. Outcomes may be similarly varied and studies of the effectiveness of social work must demonstrate the different kinds of impact it can have. These may entail changes in users' circumstances, behaviour or well being. On these changes, and on the kind of help they have received, users' perspectives must be of great significance. Also of central interest to those who provide or manage services is an understanding of their form and content and the relationship between the problems identified and the statutory responsibilities of social workers and the help given. Social work researchers must therefore take care to study what is actually delivered through social work and how, as well as its outcomes, aspirations and objectives. For good and ill social work has an impact on large and increasing number of citizens. A major aim of *Evaluative Studies in Social Work* is to increase well informed understanding of social work, based on knowledge about its real rather than imagined activities and outcomes.

The identification of effectiveness, in its various forms, can also not be the end of the story. The costs of the associated services must be studied, set in the context of their effectiveness, to allow the most efficient use of resources.

These demands present major challenges to researchers who have to use, adapt and develop a wide range of research methods and designs. Ingenuity and persistence are both required if evaluative research in social work is to be pursued in contexts often regarded as beyond the scope of such enquiry. *Evaluative Studies in Social Work* intends to make widely available not only the research findings about the impact of social work but also to demonstrate and discuss possible approaches and methods in this important and developing field of enquiry.

The first volumes in this series describe studies undertaken in the Social

Work Research Centre at the University of Stirling. The Centre is funded by the Economic and Social Research Council and the Scottish Office to evaluate the effectiveness of social work services. Later volumes may include work carried out elsewhere.

In *In Search of Prevention* Roger Fuller explores the concept of prevention in social work and reports on one of the few studies designed to evaluate the effectiveness of work which had specific preventive objectives. Bold claims are made about the capacity of social policies to prevent ill health, social disruption, family breakdown and individual suffering. Indeed, this alleged capacity may be a major justification for expenditure of public funds on health and social services. This worthy preventive aspiration also attracts much rhetoric and, on closer examination, can be seen to be shrouded in confusion. The answers to searching questions are not easily found. What, precisely, are social policies (or social work services) intended to prevent? Is there a difference between the prevention of an evil and the promotion of a good? Are the resources, knowledge and skills available equal, or even nearly equal, to the problems being tackled? Are preventive objectives sufficiently specific to allow informed judgements to be made about their achievement?

Not surprisingly social workers are at times deterred by these questions; although they may not abandon their belief in the preventive properties of their work this is not widely proclaimed or put to the test. However, here as in so many respects, social workers are not masters of their fate. At regular intervals they are enjoined by politicians and managers to prevent social ills including, in increasingly complicated welfare systems, the undesirable, albeit unintended, bad consequences which may flow from services which have different priorities and which may be uncoordinated and poorly informed. Most recently there has been great pressure on social workers to prevent long term residential care for children and custodial sentences for offenders whom, it is said, could be more appropriately and equally successfully cared for or supervised in the community.

These are quite specific preventive objectives but it is still extremely difficult to measure their attainment and therefore to reach judgements about the comparative value of different approaches in child care and the supervision of offenders. Even greater challenges are presented by the public demand, echoed in the Children Act, 1989, that through vigilance, support for families, registers, case conferences, inter-professional cooperation and so on the ill treatment and neglect of children should be prevented.

Happily social workers remain ready to rise to such challenges and, having learnt from past problems of grand goals and limited means, to plan with increasing precision their preventive roles. Increasingly too social workers want their work to be systematically evaluated, with proper account being taken not only of what they achieve but of the context of their activities, the problems they tackle and their many responsibilities. *In Search of Prevention* is one such study. It is a detailed examination of a carefully planned and executed project for children and families with extremely difficult long term problems. In the course of their work social workers defined quite precisely their preventive aims; and Roger Fuller devised a novel procedure to evaluate the achievement of the project's preventive aspirations.

The inevitable delay in the publication of research studies can sometimes reduce the value of their conclusions. This is not the case in *In Search of Prevention* and the publication of this study now is timely for several reasons. The role of voluntary agencies today in the much extolled 'mixed economy of welfare' is not well understood. *In Search of Prevention* illustrates the potential and problems of a voluntary agency in bringing together the activities of and sorting out confusions between statutory agencies. It also evaluates the impact of a carefully planned response to an enduring conundrum of social policy - its preventive capacity - which is now, once again, at the top of the social work agenda.

Juliet Cheetham

Acknowledgements

Much is owed by the author to the tolerant but critical support of colleagues at the Social Work Research Centre; to June Watson for patience and good humour in preparing the manuscript; to John Rea, sometime of Barnardo's, Scotland, who suggested the study; to the clients and professional staff who took part; and most of all to the staff of the M.A.R.S. Project.

1 Introduction

This book has two main aims. First, it describes and seeks to evaluate an example of social work practice with a 'difficult' client group - children, young people and families whose troubles have been tackled unsuccessfully by a variety of conventional social agencies. It will secondly, in documenting this practice, try to throw some light on the nature of preventive work, a term so often invoked in social work and so little defined that its use may often be put down as rhetorical. A third and subsidiary aim, but one which is necessarily bound up with the first two, is to discuss some of the methodological problems inherent in conducting an evaluative study of preventive work in a small unit whose characteristics resist traditional methods of investigation.

The origins of the study

The M.A.R.S. Project is a child care unit in the city of Dundee. It is managed by Barnardo's and jointly funded by Barnardo's and Tayside Regional Council through its education and social work departments, and had a permanent staff of three when the research was undertaken. The acronym stands for 'Mobile ... Action ... Resource ... Service', though in truth this seems often to be forgotten and bears the hallmark of something invented to fit an existing title. In former times 'Mars' was the name of

1

a nautical training school based on a ship anchored in Dundee harbour, and a small amount of money from a trust connected with the ship went into setting up the Project in 1983, which from the start had rather different aspirations from its indirect ancestor. (To compound the irony the Project was located at the time of the study in Reform Street.) The Project works intensively with children and families referred to it from a variety of statutory agencies in Dundee, notably its joint funders, the social work and education departments. Its stated aim is to forestall a major crisis or breakdown in the lives of its clients. As well as working directly with some cases, it also seeks to offer consultancy to statutory agencies and in various ways to promote inter-agency working.

A number of different kinds of interest intersect with the M.A.R.S. Project. Its client group is one notoriously resistant to 'help' and has provoked some to abandon it as a lost cause for social work. To take literally the terms of its charter, the Project aspires to work preventively by taking cases of young people who are already highly vulnerable and to arrest a further downward spiral. From a professional point of view, then, a study of the Project provides a testing ground for whether social work has an effective part to play with young people and their families whose needs are complex and challenging, and for the claims of social work to have a fruitful preventive role in helping to avert disasters threatening to overtake people already in serious difficulties.

At the same time, the Project's relationship to the local authority departments is an example of partnership between the statutory and voluntary sector, and therefore a potential model of cooperation which has gained in topicality since the study was undertaken in the late nineteen eighties. Holman (1988) has charted the struggle to secure a place for preventive work on the agenda of welfare agencies, and has argued that the role of the voluntary sector has been and will remain crucial to the preventive enterprise. In this instance, the social work and education departments of the regional council were in effect meeting two thirds of the M.A.R.S. budget, in return for what was hoped to be both a quality service provided for a relatively small number of children and families, and a wider consultancy service to the two departments. Was this way of organising a specialist child care resource a sensible arrangement for a social work department? What were its potential and its problems?

For the Social Work Research Centre, therefore, the M.A.R.S. Project offered an opportunity to explore the related issues of preventive work and the relationship between a voluntary agency and a statutory department, one a perennial question, the other of growing prominence in the organisation and deployment of the personal social services. It also met other criteria which a research unit, particularly one recently established,

2

needs to take heed of. As well as tackling a major substantive theme, a study of the M.A.R.S. Project would need to grapple with important methodological issues: notably, the degree to which the intangible concept of 'prevention' is researchable, and by what kinds of method; and the problems of studying the operation of the kind of small unit which is common in social work and which makes quantification difficult.

When a research centre has to decide what research should be undertaken, tricky pragmatic questions arise which do not always get a public airing in reports, particularly in relation to the scope of a study. In this case we were influenced by the need to establish a study quickly in the early days of the Centre. At the same time, in an era of increasing accountability even for researchers in academic units, there was the teasing issue of how much time it was reasonable to devote to a study which was bound to have a small sample, however strategically important its underlying themes, and whose subject-matter posed difficult and perhaps insoluble problems of researchability. In the end it was decided to see what could be achieved in a relatively small-scale piece of work. The fieldwork for the study occupied approximately six months, though preliminary thinking (Fuller, 1987) and subsequent analysis took somewhat longer. Although the fieldwork for the study took place in 1987-8, the practices studied have not significantly changed and the issues raised remain central to important debates about social work.

Social work, child care and prevention

As is well known, the mid-eighties saw the reporting of a wave of research studies in child care (including Millham et al, 1986; Packman et al, 1986; Fisher et al, 1986), though many of them had carried out their fieldwork a good deal earlier. These studies both reflected and contributed to a pervasive sense of disillusion about the potential of social workers to operate productively with 'troubled and troublesome' children. The findings were summarised and received apparent official endorsement (DHSS, 1985; Vernon, 1986) through a series of DHSS-sponsored seminars at which they were disseminated. The picture emerging soon became familiar: a blind progression of children and young people through various systems towards drift in long-term care; lack of planning at the individual level; response to crises; the withering of links with natural families.

The author attended one of these seminars in Scotland. It was an interesting experience to witness the mixture of responses from practitioners and managers. Scotland's different legislative arrangements for care, the distinctively prevention-focused terms of the Social Work

3

(Scotland) Act of 1968, and the children's hearing system inspire fierce loyalties among some, although it was not disputed that the adverse picture of children's experience of care was generally applicable in Scotland. What did not seem to be fully acknowledged was that the findings were by no means new or shocking, but were consistent with a body of research dating virtually from the inception of the post-Seebohm and post-Kilbrandon departments (e.g. Rowe and Lambert, 1973). Care away from home, residential care in its more custodial forms, confusions in the intersection of justice and welfare principles, the muddled history of intermediate treatment (IT), the breakdown rates of foster placements - all have been the subject of searching and often critical scrutiny.

Whatever reservations there might be about individual studies - and there are often many - the cumulative picture offered little encouragement to those who would see 'care' as a constructive and helpful means of intervention in the lives of children and their families experiencing the kinds of difficulty which lead to referral to social services or social work departments. Indeed, thoughtful social workers might be forgiven for suspecting that anything they might offer to such children and families is at risk of being contaminated by the probability of failure and by the unwieldiness of available systems for delivering 'services' which may widen the statutory net (Thorpe et al, 1980) and do more long-term harm than good.

Research findings can often be overlearnt in the field, and gloomy messages taken too much and too uncritically to heart; at the same time they can be prayed in aid along with more notorious scandals by commentators hostile to social work. Hardiker et al (1991) comment on recent trends:

> ... a retreat into technical excellence, improved professional competence, and a narrowing of the scope of social work practice. In terms of preventive services, this has meant a concentration on those children for whom long-term substitute care is unavoidable (permanency planning); on those for whom admission to care is looming, but who may be either diverted from admission (gatekeeping) or whose stay in care can be kept short and purposeful (restoration). This narrower focus has sometimes been at the expense of the more traditional family casework that first flourished in the early 1950s and on which many contemporary criticisms of social work seem to focus. (p16)

Pessimism about care (the 'last resort' fallacy) can itself be a pathological element in the system, and important arguments will continue to take place about the relative emphasis which should be placed on efforts to improve the experience of care as against attempts to divert children from it, and about the unintended consequences of doing one at the expense of the other.

These various responses, such as improving care and avoiding care, are not of course mutually exclusive. Departmental child care policy statements which proliferated in the wake of the research dissemination exercises typically give attention to all. This appears at a rhetorical level, as a commitment to the avoidance of care away from home 'when possible', and to a strict choice between rehabilitation and permanence. It is also reflected in particular mechanisms designed to improve decision-making at critical points, or 'gateposts': when entry to care is being considered, at the point of assessment, when reports are written for courts or hearings, at fixed intervals after admission, and so on. But despite all the research, which has after all been based for the most part on in-care populations, fundamental questions remain unanswered, and perhaps unanswerable. If the outcomes for children admitted to care tend to be adverse, what are the consequences for similar children who do not enter care? Are there clear indicators, recognisable to practitioners, of what kinds of problem, and at what stage, are amenable to the kinds of help practitioners have to offer? Perhaps most insistently, what if anything can be done by social workers to prevent the development of problems or circumstances which in the end make entanglement in the statutory net apparently inevitable?

The focus on decision-making (or the lack of it) and its implications for child care careers needs to be set against secular changes in the construction of child care problems and related changes in the repertoire of responses available to social agencies. These changes in professional perspective combined with changes in the financial climate in the late seventies and eighties to produce a number of new emphases in approach to child care: a stress on understanding and responding to 'problems' in the context in which they arise; a keener awareness of the capacity of agencies like schools, residential establishments, or the juvenile justice system to amplify or even to generate 'problems'; the general disrepute, on value for money as well as more purely professional grounds, of 'solutions' which involve removing children to geographically or socially remote settings.

These considerations apply to social work thinking, but are to some extent mirrored in parallel changes in the educational field. The functioning of child guidance clinics and the school psychological services in dealing with children presenting problems at school was subjected to searching criticism in the seventies (Tizard, 1973; Gillham, 1980) for the ineffectiveness of conventional modes of 'treatment' and their remoteness from the context in which problems occur. The arguments developed by Gillham (1980) for the educational psychologist to be less clinic-based, less preoccupied with individual children, and more concerned with a consultancy role in the classroom parallel the movement in social work towards making intervention more community-based.

One reading of the child care debates of the eighties would point towards considerable scepticism about the possibilities of undertaking preventive work, echoing perhaps the view of Pinker (1982) in his minority appendix to the Barclay Report: social work 'has neither the capacity, the resources, nor the mandate to go looking for needs in the community at large'. While the DHSS (1985) review is clearly unwilling to surrender the traditional preventive aspiration of social work, and Holman (1988) is a notable champion of it, others - especially those influenced by the 'systems' approach developed by Norman Tutt and his colleagues at the University of Lancaster (e.g. Bilson and Thorpe, 1987) - are more disposed to argue that early prevention is a chimera, and that preventive efforts at later stages in a child's career should be at the level of systems rather than work with individual clients, such as the creation of institutionalised gateposts or other organisational disincentives to admission, promoting the capacity of agencies other than social work to resolve their own problems, and so on.

Much, of course, turns on what is meant by the strikingly nebulous term 'prevention'. The Short Report (House of Commons, 1984), questioning the traditional over-emphasis on substitute care for children, referred by contrast to the lack of thinking and imaginative effort devoted to 'what we can only lamely call preventive work' (para 30). This uneasy sense, even among its proponents, that prevention lacks firmness of footing, and in particular that it requires clearer definition, induces wariness, particularly among researchers. The uses of the term in the mythology of social work are so often rhetorical that the task of the researcher who wishes to test its claims starts with the need to clarify the ways in which the idea of prevention may be lent a measure of realism.

Can preventive work be researched?

How can it be established that prevention has taken place? At what point in time? And what, exactly, is prevention? Consideration of the difficulties of researching prevention must start with the breadth of the concept. A large number of social work activities can in principle be included under the prevention rubric. Indeed, there seem to be few examples of social work intervention which could not be described as trying to prevent something considered undesirable. This is so whether the preventive goal (i.e. what undesirable outcome is to be prevented) is expressed in service or administrative terms (prevention of entry to care, of placement breakdown, or re-referral), or whether the goal is more personal or client-based (prevention of family breakdown, of the deterioration of relationships or behaviour).

The breadth of prevention thus produces at least a need for preventive goals to be clarified. But in addition goals are often expressed in terms which are both ambitious and intangible. Holman (1988), for example, speaks inter alia of 'preventing children enduring social disadvantage within their families'; the Seebohm report referred to the 'prevention of social distress'; the 'prevention of social breakdown' is a common formulation. (It is interesting to speculate in passing on the conceptual work being done by the prefix 'social' in these phrases. Does it have a real meaning?) For some, however, these preventive aspirations and the values they embody will be attractive; the view that a skilled and committed public service can and should tackle such evils in the lives of individuals articulates the motives many have for entering social work. Such claims, if well founded, also provide a politically defensible rationale for the public funding of social services. Their vagueness, however, is a serious problem for the fruitful discussion of prevention in practice.

In particular, it remains uncertain what manifestations of disadvantage or distress are really within the capacity of social work to grasp. When social workers had grand and ambitious targets, then tests of effectiveness were set up which they were almost bound to fail. As the profession has become more sober in its aspirations, there seems to be general agreement that, for example, homelessness, ill-health, and low incomes should be tackled in their own right by general social policies or other social agencies, and not subsumed under some giant preventive umbrella (Billis, 1984).

In this respect, the need for disaggregation, precision, and realism in the identification of preventive objectives for preventive social work coincides with the requirements of research on prevention. If the effectiveness of preventive work is to be investigated, it is clearly necessary to have specified criteria of success.

A common attempt to make the concept of preventive social work more manageable (Parker, 1980; Jones, 1985) invokes the vocabulary of health care to offer a distinction between primary, secondary and tertiary prevention. The terms 'primary', 'secondary' and 'tertiary' are usually taken to refer both to different levels of intervention, and to different stages in the sequential development of a disease or pathological condition. Thus (in health terms) primary prevention refers to preventing the emergence of a disease, by for example general improvements in basic living conditions; secondary prevention to the treatment of a disease in its early stages, to prevent it becoming a permanent disabling condition; and tertiary prevention would be directed at limiting the damaging effects of a disease once established.

If we try to apply this schema to social work, it would seem that primary prevention largely belongs in the category of abandoned ambitions referred to earlier. Social workers no longer (if they ever seriously did) see themselves as being able to influence the social-structural origins of personal troubles. (They are in an excellent position to observe and highlight their effects, and to argue for the place of primary prevention on the social policy agenda, but that is another story.) There is a seductive argument, however, that there is a 'social' equivalent to primary prevention, according to which the basic structures of family life (say) or the development of healthy attitudes to personal relationships are the social/personal equivalents of redistributed wealth or better housing. By developing strategies for improving parenting capacities for sections of the population under stress, or by seeking to enhance the power of local authorities to develop their strengths and improve their quality of life, social workers may thereby contribute to primary prevention. This seems to rest on an optimistic view, on which there may be some disagreement, of the limited armoury of social workers. Does giving a talk to fifth formers about parenting and child abuse constitute primary prevention? The validity of the argument depends on the capacity of social workers to make an impact at a level over and above that achieved with individual referred clients; whether social work, in its 'community' manifestation, has the capacity to do this is difficult to test and remains something of an article of faith among its believers.

It is in fact more usual for those interested in applying the medical metaphor to social work to take up the concepts of secondary and tertiary prevention, to which Hardiker et al (1991) add a fourth or 'quaternary' level by subdividing the tertiary stage. Using the health model, secondary prevention would consist of offering services to those who are in the early stages of a problem, or who are not (yet) 'on the books'. The intention would be either to prevent the problem becoming sufficiently serious to warrant the more drastic, costly and potentially damaging forms of intervention, or to avoid what might be defined in any given set of circumstances as 'breakdown' - or both. Tertiary prevention would assume that 'breakdown' of some sort has already occurred, but that the damaging effects (including those iatrogenic effects which flow from the intervention itself) can be mitigated.

This has the appearance of being a conceptually useful and logically viable distinction, and Hardiker et al's (1991) interesting treatment discusses these various levels of preventive intervention and their relationship to different models of welfare and their underlying value systems. However, they counsel against the fallacy of trying to locate any empirical example of preventive work too precisely in their elaborated framework of ideal types. Indeed, the difficulty lies specifically in applying these distinctions in practice; as is perhaps shown by the mediaeval disputations that can occur in discussions among theorists of prevention as to what should count as secondary and what as tertiary.

In the first place, problems experienced by the clients of social work departments come neither singly nor neatly compartmentalised. Clients are typically at different stages of involvement with a number of different agencies, and their problems are often interlaced and competing with each other for official attention or priority; what comes to be regarded as the main problem, or that which is taken up by any one agency, often has a negotiated character. Secondly, during a period of sustained social intervention, new developments are constantly occurring. Any sample of children in care of a local authority will include cases where problems in different sectors of personal life (home, siblings, school, peer group, contacts with various agencies and so on) are of different orders of seriousness and at different stages of development, and imply different styles of intervention. Such a scenario seems to cast doubt on how firmly the conceptual distinction between secondary and tertiary prevention, particularly its implied sequentiality, can be held to in practice. One might also wonder, even if used for strictly heuristic purposes, quite what conceptual advance is made: between them, secondary and tertiary prevention would seem to cover all of social work.'

Though initially promising, then, the health care analogy, from the perspective of the researcher, retains an uncomfortable element of the library rather than the real world. But what do social workers themselves mean when they speak of preventive work? Some quite particular usages are commonly deployed. One major theme among practitioners seems to be that prevention is somehow opposed to so-called statutory work, the implication being that statutory work cannot by definition be preventive. A common and related theme appears in the form of a complaint that pressure of crisis work is such that prevention is not able to force its way on to the agenda of most social workers; the implication here being that if they were able to do more preventive work then many of the crises could be averted and real advances made in the avoidance of misery, but that crisis work itself cannot be preventive. Parallel to this is a way of seeing prevention that stresses what was earlier described as a service orientation, with, perhaps increasingly, a costs perspective added: i.e. prevention as the avoidance of further penetration into what is deemed a damaging system of more and more draconian and expensive forms of intervention.

The obvious question prompted by these observations is whether social workers are here speaking of realistic options 'if only' their work could be organised differently; or whether their use of the concept really is indeed mainly rhetorical, perhaps as a handy weapon against what is seen as an intolerable level of bombardment of cases of a kind or at a stage which make it impossible to practise 'real' social work.

This discussion, which while picking up on more recent work summarises the preliminary thinking behind the case-study of preventive work which is the subject of the book, raises large questions, and larger expectations than a single piece of research can probably meet. The modest intention was that a study of the M.A.R.S. Project should contribute to thinking about preventive social work and how it may be evaluated.

Plan of the book

This chapter has set the study in context by picking out some of the related themes which underlay the study of the M.A.R.S. Project. It has also glanced at some methodological issues, which will recur constantly as the fieldwork is described and findings given.

The next chapter sets out in more detail the methodological decisions made. Chapters 3 and 4 describe the Project at work and some basic features of its collective thinking and its clientele. There follows in Chapter 5 an attempt to document systematically the Project's working methods with clients, based on the observation of sessions. Chapter 6 reports findings on effectiveness, and these are amplified in Chapter 7, which includes an extended methodological discussion of the control group dilemma and describes an experimental prediction exercise. Chapter 8 gives an account of the views concerning M.A.R.S. and its influence of the local authority social workers whose use of the Project was an important determinant of its operation. A final chapter summarises the findings briefly and discusses their implications. Case study material is scattered throughout, and also appears in an appendix.

A note on terminology

The Children Act of 1989 has altered some features of the terminology used to refer to the subject-matter of this book. Because the Act was not in force at the time the study was conducted, and does not in any case apply to Scotland, phrases such as 'children in care' have been used with their traditional meaning. For English readers, a child subject to a '44(1)(a)' order in Scotland is supervised at home by a social worker; under a '44(1)(b)' order, the child must generally be accommodated under the supervision of the social work department in a residential school or home.

There has been much discussion of the appropriate word to refer to those traditionally known as 'clients', but also from different perspectives as 'users', 'consumers' or 'customers' - particularly those whose status is not voluntary. All alternatives have their drawbacks, including their tendencies to euphemism. The author is agnostic on this point, and has tended to stick to 'client' when a term of this nature is unavoidable.

2 M.A.R.S. in context: The study design

It is an elementary truth that a study must be designed on the basis of imperfect information about the subject of the research. (If it were otherwise, of course, there would be no need to do the research.) This chapter contains some of the background information about the M.A.R.S. Project which fed into the consideration of design and methods, and a discussion of how the methodological decisions were arrived at.

The M.A.R.S. Project

At the time of the study, the Project was staffed by three full-time professional workers and a secretary, and operated from a premises situated on the top floor of a building in a row of shops and offices in central Dundee. The premises themselves consisted of two offices, for the secretary and the professional workers, a workshop, a kitchen, and a small sitting room, the latter three areas being used in various ways for working with clients. Though by no means lavish, the premises were well equipped for a variety of practical activities: woodwork and other kinds of craft work, preparing and eating a meal, computing and other games.

The Project's basic aim, as formulated in various of its documents, is 'to offer alternatives to young people in danger of being removed from their community'. M.A.R.S. is a secondary agency, in that it operates exclusively on referrals, which came mainly from the social work and education departments, but occasionally from other sources. There is no mechanism for self-referral, and no intention that there should be any drop-in or outreach component. Its target population might be variously described: a summary of the range of statements offered in sundry documents would suggest that appropriate referrals would be of children and families who were 'high risk' in terms of the range, severity and duration of their problems, and who were approaching a crisis and/or a major breakdown in their current living or schooling arrangements.

The principal services the Project described itself as offering were twofold. Direct work with children and families consisted of cases selected from among referrals as appropriate for intensive work; typically, such cases would remain with the Project for a period lasting from six months to a year, and would have once weekly sessions with one or more M.A.R.S. worker. Secondly, the Project offered a consultancy service to local professionals from the statutory sector. Both types of activity were based on a comprehensive analysis of the child's situation, the perceptions held by key parties, and the knowledge residing in the range of agencies to whom the child or family was likely to be (or to have in the past been) known. Great stress was laid on clarifying short and long-term objectives, and on securing the agreement and commitment of other professionals to these and to ongoing work.

The promise of the M.A.R.S. Project, in the light of the discussion in Chapter 1, had several dimensions. By the effort devoted to being clear and specific in its objectives, it might fill the planning vacuum identified by the child care research. Secondly, by focusing on a particularly vulnerable stage in a child's career with welfare agencies, the imminence of breakdown at home or school, it was in a position to make a reality of preventive work. Thirdly, if it proved to be effective in these efforts, it would be in part through skilled negotiation and the mobilisation of existing resources, but also in part the result of the sustained personal interaction which characterises 'traditional casework'.

The agency context

The extent to which this promise was fulfilled did not depend solely on the performance of the M.A.R.S. Project itself. It would be influenced also, and crucially, by the uses to which the Project was put through referrals and collaborative working by the main referring agencies. In order for the reader to understand the context fully brief details are given of the perspectives and policies of the local authority social work and education departments.

Social work in Dundee, the catchment area of the Project, was organised in two areas. Both areas had teams specialising in work with children, with two child care teams in each and in addition an adolescent team in one. There were also hospital-based paediatric and child psychiatry teams. A child care review team, based at headquarters in the city, carried out statutory reviews and was also represented at case conferences held at the local assessment centre. Resources for children included the residential assessment centre itself, which was said to use the Lancaster 'care and control' test (Thorpe et al, 1980) and was used as a holding and emergency placement as well as for assessment; a community-based assessment team; an IT centre; and various ad hoc IT groups. In keeping with national trends at the time, the Tayside region had been reducing its usage of residential placements, especially of the former List D schools (the Scottish equivalent of the former community homes with education). At the relevant time, the region had placed in residential settings, at 285, rather more than a quarter of its children in care; of these 37 were in List D schools. The latter figure represented a decline of approaching a half from a peak of four years previously.

The social work department's official view of the use of M.A.R.S. was contained in a memo circulated to area offices during the year prior to the study. As with many such memos it is uncertain how much it influenced practice or even how many basic grade social workers knew of its existence. (Most of those interviewed during the study did, but these tended to be staff who had actually made referrals.) The memo stated that the referral criterion should be 'cases where a child is in danger of being placed in residential care (including a List D school), where there is some possibility that additional community help might avoid this outcome'. Managers were encouraged to 'ensure that M.A.R.S. is considered by every case conference where residential care is being considered as an outcome, or before that stage is reached if appropriate'. The memo was accompanied by a statement of the Project's objectives.

The interest of the education department in M.A.R.S. must be seen in the context of the policy then developing in the department towards children experiencing difficulties during ordinary schooling. Places in special schools were declining, and the whole principle of special schooling said to be in increasing disrepute. In Dundee at the time there was one remaining List G school (or residential special school), which catered for primary and secondary age children and which offered day and residential provision; schools outside Dundee were also used.

At the same time increases in the incidence of exclusions from school were causing concern. Although most excluded pupils quickly resumed

14

their normal attendance, special mechanisms were being developed for a minority who did not. One such mechanism was a mandatory case conference in which the M.A.R.S. Project might be involved. Another was a burgeoning system of 1:1 teaching arrangements. Initially instituted with rigorous selection criteria, specifying that it should only be used as part of a programmed plan to reintegrate children into mainstream education, the phenomenon had become more common and perhaps less closely controlled than originally envisaged. This view, reported by a member of the education department in an interview, was supported by the fact that figures for the number of children receiving 1:1 teaching in Dundee were hard to come by: the respondent's estimate was 50. It would have been unusual for this to be full time. There had also been developed in conjunction with this arrangement the notion of an educational package, often multi-disciplinary, for those having schooling problems. This might consist of a mixture of 1:1 teaching, work experience, sessions in the mainstream school, and supportive work with something like the M.A.R.S. Project, varied in different ways according to the needs of individual cases. As an independent body, M.A.R.S. was seen as having an important role in devising and/or implementing 'packages' and especially, since in most cases there was likely to be statutory social work involvement, in bridging any gaps in communication or collaboration between the two local authority departments.

A second educational route of entry to M.A.R.S., which might overlap with the first, was via the educational social work (ESW) service, in Tayside located within the education department. ESWs engaged with children at risk of removal to residential forms of education provision were encouraged to consider referrals to the Project.

As in the social work department, though in somewhat different terms, there was an internal memo circulated to headteachers setting out the M.A.R.S. referral criteria. In this instance the memo enclosed a document produced by the Project, stating that M.A.R.S. offered 'individual programmes aimed at reintegrating children who have difficulties in school or in getting to school or who are being considered for special education'. It was also specified that the child would have 'exhausted the usual resources of the referring agency'. The 'usual resources' might be expected to include internal school procedures, meetings between heads and parents, exclusion, and, if repeated, a case conference involving an educational psychologist and an ESW. It would be at this point that a referral to M.A.R.S. could be considered.

It will be seen that the guidance given to its staff by the education department was somewhat more specific than that given to social workers, in that it stressed prior attempts to resolve problems by conventional resources. This emphasis accurately reflected the concerns of Project staff to avoid both early intervention of a net-widening kind and being seen as a substitute for thoughtful and imaginative efforts by statutory workers. That teachers were warned more forcibly of this than their social work counterparts may be mildly puzzling, though perhaps too much weight should not be attached to the wording of departmental memos, especially as their degree of actual influence is uncertain!

The design of the study

The particular methodological challenges presented by a study of the M.A.R.S. Project were the more important in that they stem from features commonly found in social work, especially in its more intensive forms. The Project dealt with a small number of cases at any one time, which makes quantification on the basis of a sample of cases problematic without a long period of study during which such a sample might be recruited. In most circumstances this would be unrealistic, not only for the length of time that would have to be devoted to the research, but also because, in the nature of this kind of enterprise, the intervention itself is likely to change over a period of prolonged study, so that later recruits to the sample would not undergo the same experience as those joining earlier.

This consideration pointed to a small sample, in the interests of methodological realism. This in itself creates difficulties for a conventional research design, which might, for example, involve comparing outcomes for sampled cases with those for a matched control group of cases not referred to the Project. In the first place, satisfactory matching would be extremely difficult to achieve, given the M.A.R.S. referral criteria: cases would have to be matched not only on personal characteristics but also on features of their previous careers. Secondly, the smaller the compared samples the more tentative would be the conclusions that could be drawn. Thirdly, regardless of sample size there are acknowledged difficulties in these research circumstances in controlling the 'process variables': i.e. in determining that the precise components of the intervention will differ consistently from what happens in the comparison group. If this is not done, the requirements of the classic experimental design will not be satisfied (cf the celebrated arguments of Cornish and Clarke 1972). This debate is entered more fully in Chapter 7.

There is a further set of considerations, however, which even without the above, and despite the esteem in which the experimental model of evaluation is held among researchers and lay people alike, should make one pause. In the M.A.R.S. style of intervention, as with many other social work services, the clientele may be assumed to be heterogeneous: the referral criteria were sufficiently loose to allow for a wide variety of 'problems' and previous histories. As a result, we should expect that the methods of intervention, the individual objectives, and the desired outcomes will also be heterogeneous. Indeed, as we have seen, the Project laid great stress on the individually tailored programmes of intervention that are devised. Methods, objectives, and outcomes were likely to vary in degree of complexity, in breadth of focus, in the time deemed necessary for their accomplishment; in a word they were likely to be non-standardisable. It is difficult to see how a single (or even a complex) measure of outcome, of the kind needed for meaningful comparisons, could have been validly applied across a sample of cases. Furthermore, the sheer intractability of the kinds of problems typically taken up by social work cast some doubt on the realism of over-arching service objectives like avoiding entry to care. The optimum outcome may simply be utopian for many clients whose lives are beset by problems on which social work can make only marginal impact.

Once 'problems' are disaggregated, so too are potential solutions. A researcher has two options in this situation. One is to seek rigorous specification, in the construction of a sample, of the problems being tackled, to ensure that a global outcome measure or measures is appropriate. The second is to accept the heterogeneity and to seek a solution to the technical problem of non-standardisable outcomes. This issue has arisen especially, for example, in research which has sought to study the effectiveness of assessment processes, where outcomes clearly cannot be looked at without taking account of the differences between individuals which are identified in assessment (Fuller 1985).

One solution to this can take the form of measuring outcomes by the achievement of distinctive objectives set in individual cases, and adopting some means of aggregating these to obtain an overall effectiveness rating for the service under investigation. This was among the methods used by Rowe et al (1989) in their study of patterns and outcomes in a large sample of child care placements in six local authorities. Thus as well as measuring the length of placements the researchers obtained social workers' judgements on whether placements had lasted as planned, less than planned, or longer than planned; whether they lasted as needed, less than needed, or longer than needed; and to what extent, on a four-point scale, they had achieved the 'primary aim' of the placement (e.g. 'temporary care', 'treatment', 'assessment', 'bridge to independence'). Somewhat tentatively, the researchers go on to derive a composite measure of overall placement 'success': a placement was deemed successful if it was rated as (a) lasting as long as needed and (b) meeting the aim fully or

17

in most respects.

Though said by the authors to be a crude undertaking, this nonetheless enables a degree of disaggregation in a sample likely to be composed of widely differentiated sub-groups. One problem, however, is that Rowe et al's method permits only a single 'primary' objective to be selected for each case, lending an unrealistically unidimensional character to the professional input.

A bleak inference from the rehearsal of these difficulties would be that a venture like M.A.R.S. is impossible to evaluate - at least without doing violence to its nature - by other than impressionistic means. If such a conclusion is warranted, the consequences are quite serious for the prospects of scrutinising critically, on the basis of objective evidence, large and important areas of social work activity. The experience of the Social Work Research Centre (Cheetham et al, 1992) is that there are no magic solutions to the problems of conducting evaluative research in social work; rather it is on the whole a matter of applying and adapting, in a pragmatic spirit, a range of established methods of social research. The study was designed in part to explore the possibility of developing a method of examining preventive objectives and outcomes in a relatively brief investigation.

Research questions and methods

The overall aims of the study were to document the effectiveness of the M.A.R.S. Project by examining a sample of its cases and the uses made of the Project by statutory agencies. These broad aims were broken down into more specific questions:

1. **What is M.A.R.S.?** What are its professional resources? How do staff view their general aims, their clientele, their relationship with other agencies, their methods of working? What are their methods in practice?

2. **Who goes to M.A.R.S.?** What sort of children and young people are referred, with what problems and at what stage in their careers? Do referred cases correspond to the M.A.R.S. view of their target group?

3. **What is the impact of M.A.R.S. on children and families?** To what extent are objectives and methods modified during intervention? What are the outcomes of intervention as indicated by placement stability, prevention of identified risk, perceptions of M.A.R.S. staff, statutory

workers, and clients?

4. **What is the impact of M.A.R.S. on local agencies?** Do local
professionals value the Project, and in what ways? Are referrers aware
of any impact on their own patterns of working? Do M.A.R.S. staff or
local managers see any impact on general patterns of working?

In general these questions were to be addressed by qualitative means
and in a pluralistic (Smith and Cantley, 1984) spirit. A range of
perspectives would be sought, with a major reliance on interviews with
Project staff, with referrers and other professionals, and with clients.
Monitoring the progress of individual cases would be as prospective as
feasible, given the constraints of the study's duration, in order to enhance
the reliability of the accounts given.

Sample

The main sample was to consist of direct work cases drawn from recent
and current referrals. The criteria for inclusion were a referral date from
a six-month period prior to fieldwork and during the six months of
fieldwork itself. It was hoped thus to maximise the numbers of completed
cases while avoiding too great a retrospective element. Data was also to
be gathered on consultancy cases referred during the period of the study.

Data collection

The main means of data collection was the semi-structured interview. The
M.A.R.S. staff were interviewed on several occasions, both in a group and
individually, about their general approach and about individual cases in the
sample. Their records were also drawn upon to supplement the interview
material and for background information about the Project. Referrers and
their immediate managers were interviewed for information about cases
in the sample, their expectations and views of outcome; about the
experience and impact of working with the Project; and about their views
on its overall effectiveness. Clients from the direct work sample were
interviewed (both children and their parents) about what they saw as the
purposes of the M.A.R.S. involvement, their experiences of the Project, its
strengths and weaknesses, and whether and in what ways they thought they
had benefitted from it.

In addition the author spent time in the Project observing day-to-day
procedures and attending key meetings. A more systematic period of
observation was spent in Project working sessions with three individual

clients from the direct work sample. One purpose of this was simply to document the working methods of the Project; a second, however, was to give the reader the opportunity to assess the appropriateness of the methods of working to the goals pursued, and thus increase the face plausibility of the findings.

Outcomes

Outcomes of work with the clients in the direct work sample were to be measured by the identification of individual objectives and an assessment, through interviews with staff, clients and referrers, of the extent to which they had been achieved over a period. Ideally this period would coincide with the total duration of a case, but it was recognised that this might not be possible in all cases because of the unpredictable length of the involvement. Difficulties were also likely to arise if objectives evolved significantly during the life of a case. It was nevertheless hoped that the study would provide the opportunity to develop thinking about characteristic preventive objectives for wider application.

Validity

Indicators of 'success' independent of the perceptions of interested parties were likely to be available only rarely, such as in those instances where an objectively determinable outcome like a change of placement was in question - and even here there was no guarantee that the meaning attached should be unambiguously that of success or failure. This reinforced the need for all the relevant parties to be interviewed.

An additional area of uncertainty was that involved in ascribing the achievement of objectives specifically to the intervention of the Project, rather than coming about through some other process, either spontaneously or because of some other non-M.A.R.S. intervention. This question, precisely that which a control group would at any rate purport to address, was to be tackled through a methodological experiment, the use of prediction. The plan was to assemble a group of independent assessors, who would be shown case-histories of individuals referred to M.A.R.S. up to the point of referral; they would then be asked to predict the likely outcome of these cases given the conventional resources of social work only, i.e. without the availability of the distinctive M.A.R.S. style of intervention. Any difference between the hypothetical outcomes, as predicted, and the actual outcomes would (assuming a degree of consensus among the predictors) would be hypothesised to be a measure of the impact of the Project's work with the case. The use of panels of assessors

20

is not unknown in social work research (e.g. Thorpe et al, 1980) but the device did not appear to have put in the past to precisely this use.

Difficulties encountered

As will emerge, some of these research aims evolved as the study developed, and others became problematic at an early stage.

The permission of the local social work department to interview social workers and elicit data on clients had of course been sought during preliminary negotiations. After the study had been designed, however, it became clear that access to file data on individual clients would only be made available on certain conditions. The policy of the department was that before any information held by the department about clients could be divulged, the informed and written consent of the client should first be obtained by social work staff. This policy, though not specifically oriented towards researchers, has serious implications for research. In this instance, the proposal to attend referral meetings and observe the M.A.R.S. information-gathering procedures came into question, as these would often take place within a matter of days following the notification of the referral. When this dilemma was put to senior managers, it was suggested that the research needs could be met by social workers obtaining permission from the client at the same time as their approval was sought to make the M.A.R.S. referral. This seemed too fallible a procedure to work effectively. That part of the research aimed at examining the referral process, therefore, was confined to a study of the M.A.R.S. records, the Project having an open access policy for its files. As a result, data on the referral, information-gathering, and decision-making processes - an important forum for the discussion and exploration of inter-agency issues - were of a more second-hand character than had originally been hoped.

A second difficulty arose from the method used to identify the sample of direct work cases. The initial plan had been to draw the sample from three periods: all those who were clients of M.A.R.S. at the start of the fieldwork; those who had been taken on during the previous six months; and those taken on during the six months of the fieldwork. It had been estimated on the basis of information supplied beforehand that this would yield a sample of approaching twenty cases. In the event the numbers were less than this (see the next chapter), and even after extending the retrospective element of sample recruitment by going back in time beyond the previous six months the final sample was only twelve cases. The implication of this was that the pattern of working had undergone changes during the planning stages of the study, resulting in a lower turnover of cases at the Project. Alternatively, this could be yet another example of researchers and practitioners colluding to over-estimate the flow of referrals - while it is very common to read in a research report that the sample was smaller than hoped, the opposite is rarely encountered!

3 M.A.R.S. at work: An overview

This chapter fills out the picture provided earlier about the Project's resources and procedures. Its general approach will be described, followed by an overview of the flow of work during the six-month period of fieldwork.

Resources

It goes without saying that its three social work staff, together with the Project secretary, constituted the most important of the M.A.R.S. resources. No doubt this is true of any social work agency; it cannot fail to be so in a setting with such a high proportion of intensive personal work.

The Project leader was a qualified social worker, who had been with M.A.R.S. for four years. Before that she had had ten years' field experience in social work departments, including four years as a senior. The second worker had been with M.A.R.S. for one year, after four years' experience as a specialist social worker in mental health and child psychiatry teams and six years in residential work (List D and List G schools). The third worker had been in post for six months, and was qualified in general and psychiatric nursing, with two years' nursing experience and four years in residential social work. There was thus a considerable degree of varied professional experience in the team, though it was acknowledged by all members that the third worker had less relevant experience and might have greater needs for support. The greater part of the Project's budget went towards staff salaries.

The physical plant has already been described. In addition to permanent features of the premises, there was considerable freedom to purchase items used in practical activities such as woodwork projects, on food for preparation and consumption on the premises, and on meals out with clients. The most outstanding single item of expenditure of this kind during the study was probably the financial assistance given to a family for a Barnardo's-organised group holiday in Spain for a week. When asked about this in a group interview, the Project leader commented that 'materially we're not constrained at all ... we're very fortunate'.

The M.A.R.S. procedures

In principle, the Project responded to the referrals it received in one of two ways: by providing **direct** work, where a 'contract' was offered and accepted and where individual work took place with a client; and through indirect or **consultancy** work, a kind of specialist advisory service to social workers and other professionals which might not include any face-to-face contact with the client. In practice the difference between these categories was not as clear-cut as this might suggest. An account of how incoming work might find its way into one or the other is best given through a description of typical procedures, or the 'natural history' of a referral.

Following receipt of a referral, which might be by telephone and which would include brief details, a **referral meeting** would be arranged, attended by all project staff, the referrer, and (in the case of the latter being a social worker) the referrer's senior. There were no standard referral forms. At this stage, the referrer might be seeking consultancy, be asking the Project to 'take' the case for direct work, or might have no clear idea in mind. At the referral meeting, the decision would be made whether or not to go to the next standard stage, known as **information-gathering.** The client's permission having been obtained, Project staff would visit all the agencies who had had contact with the client, sometimes reaching far back into the past, in order to obtain a clear picture of the work that had been done and of different parties' understanding of the case. This phase would often identify inter-agency issues that might need to be addressed, and might last a period of some three weeks. There followed a **feedback meeting** with the referrers at which a decision would be made whether to take the case for direct work, or 'offer a contract': if so, the client would be approached by Project staff, usually for the first time.

Just as there was no referral document, there was no standard form for recording the decision or the objectives identified at the feedback meeting. Instead, written minutes of these meetings were produced, and these constituted the statement of objectives and the 'contract'. In fact, although the term was freely used by Project staff, this was not a contract in the usual social work sense: although there seemed to be some ambiguity about this, the contract was generally an agreement between the Project and the referrer rather than with the client, and would usually incorporate an agreed and clearly spelled out division of tasks and roles between M.A.R.S. staff and the other agencies involved.

Thus in order for a case to achieve direct work or contract status, a number of procedures were gone through. At any stage in the sequence of events, however, it might be decided that the case was for whatever reason not appropriate for a contract. Indeed some cases could be screened out informally without reaching a referral meeting. (This raises questions, further explored in Chapter 8, about potential referrers' knowledge of the referral criteria and about the clarity of these criteria.) The term consultancy tended to be used by Project staff to cover all cases which were discussed, to whatever stage, but which did not reach contract status. As such, consultancy was something of a catch-all or residual category. It included a range of quite different types of referral episode: cases where the intention of the referrer was for no more than discussion; where the referrer had no explicit intentions; where the M.A.R.S. staff were unwilling or unable to offer a contract; where the client was unwilling to work with the Project. There were also cases which appeared to have an intermediate character, where direct work with the client took place on a strictly limited basis while a specifically agreed assessment was carried out on behalf of or in collaboration with the referrer. An intermediate case of this kind could last as long as a full direct work case where for some reason the work proved to be abortive and contact was prematurely terminated - a rare but not unknown event.

There were other opportunities for M.A.R.S. staff to provide consultancy. In one of the social work areas of Dundee there was a regular meeting of a 'resource group' comprising area middle management, residential and IT staff, and attended by a Project worker, at which cases of children at risk of admission to care or posing particular difficulties were discussed. Project staff would also attend other meetings on a more ad hoc basis.

Non-contract work was therefore rather a mixed bag. Its heterogeneous nature, and the negotiated character of the distinctions between it and contract work, posed difficulties for the aim originally envisaged of comparing the characteristics of direct cases and those of consultancy cases. This was compounded by the nature of the M.A.R.S. records, which did not contain systematic details of the case-histories of referrals. Project records were constructed on the basis of information and analysis/synthesis, gleaned during referral procedures, and additional to information already held: items such as placement history and previous episodes of care and supervision were believed to be properly located in the social work file, the M.A.R.S. file containing only those features considered relevant to the current deliberations. Project staff were quite clear about the professional rationale for this, but it posed problems for the researcher without access to other agencies' records. A systematic comparison between direct and consultancy cases was not in the end attempted.

Once a case had been accepted for direct work, the patterns of engagement were quite fluid and sometimes collective. It was possible for one Project member to be the designated worker on a particular case, but equally possible for two or even all three to work jointly on different or even on the same aspects of the agreed programme of work; and this could change as the case developed. During the fieldwork, there were regular internal meetings of various kinds (individual supervision, group supervision, review meetings) which seemed to ensure that all staff were reasonably well-informed about the state of all live cases.

This description of the referral processes might give the impression that a referred case had to surmount a series of hurdles in order to reach the contract stage. While this would be misleading, since neither referrers nor Project staff assumed that the only or optimal use of M.A.R.S. was for direct work, it does raise the question of the ways in which the Project structured its actual and potential workload. Some indications of how this worked out in practice may be gleaned from the remainder of this chapter and the following.

General approach

The general aproach of the Project was explored in lengthy group interviews with staff, with the aim of eliciting their ways of constructing the field of activity, or 'ideology in practice' (Giller and Morris 1981). Although (as might be expected) the most prominent contributor to the discussions was the Project leader, the impression was one of broad consensus between staff, albeit with some individual differences of approach which were evidently well established in the group and respected.

Questions were asked about the extent to which the Project was guided by social work theory. What constitutes a theory in this context is perhaps a moot point, but the significance for the present purpose lies in what the staff believed to be their guiding principles. The M.A.R.S. philosophy was said not to derive from a single, overarching perspective, but to include a number of theoretical strands. Those mentioned were 'community development', 'task-centred work', 'the Lancaster work on gate-keeping', and 'systems theory'. The author was rather puzzled by the reference to community development, which was explained as

> a basic difference in attitudes to people between a community worker and a social worker ... a social worker sees people in terms of their problems and what help they need ... whereas a community worker sees them in terms of their positives ... we see them as having a great deal of potential. A basic theory of this Project is that people can change, anyone can change.

The context here made it clear that the 'people' who could change included not only clients but also professional staff who might be brought to alter their ways of working with clients. Similarly, systems theory seemed to be interpreted as a rationale for the Project's work with other agencies: area social work teams, schools, children's homes, and so on. (For another practitioner's contrasting view of systems theory, see Chapter 8.) The staff saw themselves as being task-centred in their emphasis on clarifying objectives and setting time-limits, an emphasis which in fact seemed to be more apparent in the early and consultancy stages than in direct work as it developed, where it was freely acknowledged that there was a considerable degree of open-endedness in the commitment. The language used to describe direct work included 'traditional casework' and 'family therapy'. The latter term was clearly employed as a form of shorthand to denote intensive work with families: Project staff would claim some acquaintance with family therapy theories and techniques, but were fully aware that they were not trained therapists.

This eclecticism needs some comment. One staff member put it like this:

> I would say that the Project draws on a whole range of theories ... we don't have a specific method that we apply ... we prepare a programme for the individual situations that we're dealing with, and we then have to draw on all sorts of different methods of actual work.

One could interpret these responses to questions about theory in various ways. It could be taken, at face value, as evidence of the degree to which

M.A.R.S. workers were aware of and followed certain social work theories, and assessed accordingly. Although, compared with the theoretical unawareness among social workers reported by such as Browne (1978), this group of specialists would probably have scored relatively highly, there was an element of picking and choosing from different theoretical perspectives which might be held by purists to run counter to the exigencies of any one of them. To social work educators, too, it might be chastening to note that familiarity with particular theories is partly a function of the date at which staff are trained. Against this, however, it might be argued that a pragmatic eclecticism was entirely appropriate given uncertainty in the field about ends and means, and the multiplicity of situations and problems met in the Project.

This does not seem, however, to take us very far in seeking to identify the M.A.R.S. principles in practice. Somewhat closer to the ground was the way in which these abstract views of theory took their significance from, and merged into, two more concrete areas. The first was the perceived difference between the position of the M.A.R.S. workers and that of their statutory sector counterparts. The second related to the nature of the demand for M.A.R.S. as expressed in the type (as staff saw it) of referrals received.

Thus remarks about theory and method were often linked with statements - some no doubt contentious - about the relatively disadvantageous position of the statutory workers:

> I would challenge, from the evidence we have of working with them, that social workers who say they are influenced by systems theory are in fact able to practice it ... they're not given the time or the training ...

This was developed into a picture of a statutory social work service operating under conditions, mainly of workload and bureaucratic constraint, which made good social work extremely difficult to practice. The M.A.R.S. staff, while acknowledging that many statutory workers were skilled and effective, saw themselves as being unusually fortunate in enjoying the time, resources, support, and freedom from constraint that enabled them to make their distinctive contribution. As the Project leader commented 'when social workers say "it's all very well for you", that's exactly what I've said, it is all very well for us'. This view of the statutory sector was a powerful influence on how Project staff saw their role and function:

> a large part of why the Project works is opportunity of time and space,

and that is in terms of limiting the number of kids, and having the office here to work with youngsters or families, and the resource we have ... we're not hampered by stupid applications for money to do something, we can just make our minds up to do something at lunch-time today and go out and do it.'

Overall, the blend in particular of **time** and related **freedoms from constraint** proved to be a central underlying theme of the study.

The second area which seemed to act as a bridge between theory and practice, and which was also linked to perceptions of the statutory sector, was the the Project's view of the kind of referrals received. One discussion of the nature of preventive work had focused initially on the Project's stated criteria for referral. This soon became an account of what were seen as 'subtle changes' in the pattern of referrals being received. Instead of children who were purely at risk of imminent major breakdown, it had been observed that increasing numbers of referrals were of those for whom appropriate resources were not available: 'being sent home inappropriately, being placed inappropriately in the assessment centre, referrals for failed placement, kids in limbo...'

This was agreed to imply a less definable kind of role for M.A.R.S. and some concern was expressed, though of a tentative and ambiguous kind:

The issue that concerns me most about these placement breakdowns is that there's a lack of skill in the management of these cases ... does the problem lie in lack of resources, or in lack of skill in management or in the workers? Or is it in pulling it all together?

It was difficult to say whether this represented a real change in the nature of referrals: the point being made rests on an elusive distinction. For the Project, however, the force of the observation was to highlight particular intepretations of their role in relation to the statutory agencies.

These perspectives, and the uncertainties with which they were expressed, would seem to suggest possible explanations for some features of the M.A.R.S. procedures which might otherwise have seemed puzzling. The slightly unusual way in which the term 'contract' was used, with some ambiguity as to whether the second party was the client or the referrer, has already been noted. The agreements which formed the basis of the intervention were often more specific in respect of the roles of M.A.R.S. staff and the referrers than of expectations of clients. One staff member actually commented, semi-seriously, that 'our real client sometimes is the worker'. The initial information-gathering process could also be re-interpreted in light of this. Project staff were reluctant to use the expected term 'assessment' to describe that stage, in the belief that to do so would give the misleading impression that the individual child was being assessed: 'we very specifically don't do that, we are taking in everyone else around the child and the situation...'. In fact, as has been described, the individual child was not actually seen until the information-gathering and analysis were complete and the contract offered. It might also seem that the nominal client was in some sense of secondary importance to the assessment of previous intervention and the totality of the possibly fragmented information that could be put together: 'the rationale is that we do the analysis with the professionals about what they've done'.

We may also account for what seemed to some of the statutory sector staff a problematic feature of the M.A.R.S. approach, their insistence on continuing to share responsibility for a case rather than taking it over completely. The policy was to 'include them in what we're doing, not to take the case away but to actually involve them in what we're doing or discussing or whatever ... and leave some skills with them'.

It might well be imagined that this aspect of the M.A.R.S. approach was likely to provoke some reaction from the statutory professionals. Most of the points made here will re-appear in Chapter 8.

There remains one further aspect of the Project's general approach which should be mentioned here. It was understood that M.A.R.S. would not accept a case which they believed could be adequately dealt with by the referring agency, i.e. which in layman's terms was too 'easy'. Staff were asked, conversely, whether there any kinds of case which they would regard as inappropriate because they were too 'difficult'.

Responses to this were complex. At first a reply was given in terms of the 'severity of the damage': there were some children so damaged that they required a specialised, especially psychiatric, input, or that they were unable to respond in a 1:1 relationship to an adult. A slightly different group would be those where the power of their own subculture was so great that any intervention was impotent. This position was subsequently elaborated further, in a discussion of the pros and cons of early and late intervention, by reference to the type of 'damage'. This developed into a distinction between those children who were the victims of clumsy or inappropriate intervention - and who responded to that in their behaviour - and those who were 'more damaged' in some profound personal sense. While the former were seen as the Project's ideal target group, staff accepted a role with the latter, even if chances of success were remote, if only to help establish the nature of the problems.

The flow of work over six months

Information concerning unevenly moving 'stocks and flows', as with social workers' caseloads, is always difficult to present clearly. At any given point, workers will have a number of live cases, of differing points of origin in the past. During any given period subsequent to that point, some of these cases will be closed, some will remain open, and new ones will have been taken on. At M.A.R.S. this moving picture of the workload, already rather confusing, was made more so by the fact that the Project dealt with cases at two distinct levels, that of direct work with clients and that of consultancy; furthermore, as we have seen, the latter category was not particularly clearcut, and there was also an intermediate category, of work which might be either 'limited direct' or extended consultancy.

Preliminary information had suggested that at any one point there were likely to be from ten to twelve cases of direct work being undertaken, and that the intervention with these cases might last up to a year. There were thus (at least) two factors influencing the flow of work: the rate at which referrals deemed appropriate came in; and the number of slots available to the Project staff, given that the expected time commitment made to a contract case would be one or more half-day sessions per week. There might well be some interaction between these two factors; that is, the decision as to which cases met the criteria and were appropriate to take on might be influenced to some extent by the availability of slots - a delicate balance to be struck in a unit of this type, which cannot afford to appear under-utilised.

During the six months of the study period, the Project handled in various ways a total of 34 cases, some already live at the start of the period, others new referrals. Of these, 13 were the subject of direct work and 21 of other less intensive kinds of input. The initial exploration of the work of the Project revealed that the start date happened to coincide with a period, then coming to an end, during which referrals had been rather thin. As a result there were somewhat fewer active direct cases (eight, of which one was shortly to be closed) than was said to be the norm. In addition there were a number of referrals (four) awaiting initial discussions and investigations.

In the six months in which work was monitored, there were 22 new referrals, in addition to the four cases pending at the start. Of these 26 cases which could potentially become direct or contract cases, five were offered contracts and became the subject of intensive intervention by the Project. A further three received various forms of short-term but active input. The remainder either did not get beyond the referral meeting and analysis stage, for one reason or another, or were still under consideration when the monitoring period finished. During the six months three direct cases were closed, of which one was subsequently reopened, and a further case was all but closed. This somewhat confusing information is summed up in Table 3.1.

Table 3.1
Flow of work over 6 months

'Contract' cases at start	8
Referrals pending at start	4
New referrals	22
All referrals:	
offered contracts	5
received short-term work	3
'consultancy' only/decision pending	18
'Contract' cases closed	3
Total dealt with	34

It will be seen that the direct work caseload did indeed hover around the figure of ten or a dozen during the period, in other words that the apparent under-use of the M.A.R.S. resource at the start was made up quite quickly. The phenomenon of the thin period of referrals did however have unfortunate consequences for the study, since it had been decided to use the direct work cases as the main sample. The low initial numbers meant both that the sample of cases for detailed study was smaller than had originally been hoped, and that fewer of these cases had run their full course before the end of the study period.

Of course there were activities other than those related to incoming referrals which were occupying the time of the M.A.R.S. staff during this period. There was a trickle of demands for Project staff to contribute to various training exercises in Tayside and elsewhere, which were seen as a significant part of their role. A special factor operating at the time was the preparation needed for the impending arrival of seconded staff from the education and social work departments, which included the need for the Project leader to consider the likely changes in her role and her probable reduced capacity to engage in casework, and the need to find new and larger premises.

The next chapter will describe on more detail the children and families who went to M.A.R.S.

4 The clients

In describing the users of the Project, we face a common dilemma. The clients of social work agencies are generally described in terms of the problems perceived by the professionals and the partial solutions they feel able to offer - hence, as is widely acknowledged, the potentially pathologising tendency to define clients in terms of these 'problems' and 'solutions' which is difficult to avoid. Accounts of the difficulties experienced by clients of a welfare agency are inevitably set in the context of larger accounts of the purposes of the agency as interpreted by its staff and the way they see the reasons for clients becoming clients - not all of which is made explicit. The M.A.R.S. staff were well aware of a tendency for reification and stereotyping inherent in the vocabulary of 'problems'; indeed this is part of their rationale for taking a fresh and probing look at the cases referred, with a view, among other things, to identifying positive features which might offset the negatives accentuated in the referral career.

It is thus hard to get directly at the reality of the client's situation. To mitigate the difficulties, material in the second part of this chapter is drawn from interviews with M.A.R.S. staff and their records, but also from interviews with referrers and those clients who agreed to an interview. It is not easy, however, especially in this context where emphasis is laid on arriving collectively at an agreed approach, to know how to interpret consensus about problem definition and case objectives. It could be a tribute to the success of the intensive negotiating process embodied in the M.A.R.S. referral procedures as much as a reflection of the reliability of the assessments made.

With these caveats, the chapter will give limited basic data about cases referred, their problems, and the broad objectives set in direct work cases. Examples are also given of consultancy work.

Cases referred: basic data

It will be remembered that during the study period the Project handled 13 direct work cases and that there were 21 'other' referrals; the majority of the latter were the subject of various forms of consultancy, but some were being considered for direct work contracts at the close of the period. Basic data are given in tables 4.1, 4.2 and 4.3 about both categories of referral.

Table 4.1
Sex of children referred

	direct work	other/pending
boys	9	16
girls	3	4
n/a (parent/family)	1	1

An immediate question arises as to the identity of the client: while in some cases this was clearly the individual child referred, in others it was variously the family as a whole, the parent(s), or it might be that the focus over time was shifting or equivocal. For the sake of simplicity, information in the tables is given about the individual child to whom the referral was attached, with the proviso that this may be somewhat artificial.

Table 4.2
Age of children referred

	direct work	other/pending
10 years or less*	3	3
11-13 years	3	5
14-15 years	6	12
n/a (parent/family)	1	1

* In the youngest category, the focus of work turned out eventually to be with the family as a whole in two of the three direct work cases.

Table 4.3
Source of referral

	direct work	other/pending
SWD (area)	7	18
SWD (hospital)	1	-
ESW	2	1
school	2	-
educational psychologist	1	1
consultant psychiatrist	-	1

Table 4.3 shows the referral sources actually noted for the cases, but to give a single referral source is sometimes misleading, given the multi-

disciplinary context in which referrals might be made. A referral might be suggested at a case conference (as with at least one of the 'school referrals') or following less formal discussions between professionals. For this reason Table 4.3 underestimates the extent to which the educational psychology and child psychiatric services were involved in promoting the use of M.A.R.S. as a resource. Despite this, however, it is clear that the social work department was the main source of referrals to the Project, and many were at the sole instigation of social workers in consultation with their seniors. While age or sex do not seem to differentiate the two categories, the social work department dominates the 'other/pending' column. There was probably a twofold explanation for this. The social workers were indeed making relatively greater use of M.A.R.S. for the purposes of consultancy, but in addition they were approaching the Project in a more open-ended way - referrers from the education department were more likely to come to M.A.R.S. with an already worked out package. It may have been, also, that the social workers were making more referrals deemed inappropriate.

Further systematic comparison of the two groups is obviously limited by the small numbers and the lack of systematic information, but one suspects that in any case the distinctions between cases accepted for direct work and 'others' would remain a shadowy area. What was involved were judgements made by M.A.R.S. staff about the appropriateness of the referral problem, interacting with further judgements about the ability of the Project to work constructively in the environment formed by the agency already in contact and its intervention. Some of the Project's professed criteria for making these judgements have been discussed in the previous chapter. Some brief examples follow of 'other' or non-direct work of different kinds, which nonetheless occupied a significant proportion of Project time.

A limited commitment

Danny (aged 13) was referred by his social worker. Problems were identified as school behaviour, relationships in the family, and 'soiling and wetting'. He was at the assessment centre, after showing behaviour problems in a children's home. During the referral and feedback meetings, the Project view, that Danny should not be returned home, was in the minority. It was agreed that a month should be spent with the joint involvement of M.A.R.S. and the social worker, investigating Danny's mother's commitment to having her son at home and monitoring his school attendance. The M.A.R.S. activity was to help in the analysis of taped joint interviews with the mother, and to attend meetings held in the school.

This, probably best described as an extended period of assessment, came to an end after the agreed month.

A commitment cut short

Richard, an infant, was referred by his social worker. His father was about to return home from prison, and there was concern about possible abuse. The worker was uncertain about whether this family should be reunited, and whether intervention in the family would reduce the risk. The Project agreed to undertake some family work, but before this could take place relations between the parents deteriorated and they split up.

Consultancy

Jeff (aged 15 and resident at a children's home) was referred by his social worker following aggressive behaviour and offences. After detailed discussion of the situation, it was agreed that there were ways of handling this short of Project involvement, but a contingency plan was made for M.A.R.S. to become involved if there was a return home to Jeff's mother and the placement needed support.

The first two of these examples were on the books for a period of weeks only, and the third was dealt with at the one referral meeting: as such they represented a fair selection of non-direct work. The duration of direct cases, where involvement was generally longer and more intensive, is set out in Table 4.4.

Table 4.4
Duration of direct work cases

	cases closed	cases open (at end of fieldwork)
1-6 months	1	4
7-12 months	2	2
> 13 months	-	3

(From this point on the data about direct cases will refer to the study sample of 12 cases, one of the overall total of 13 having been excluded as its closure was imminent at the start of fieldwork.)

What is noticeable here, even with the small numbers, is the unevenness. The cases of longest standing were still active at the end of the study period - this may suggest a bi-polar distribution, with a tendency for cases to be either closed after a few months or to remain open for a year or more. It could however be an effect of the anomalously thin period just before the start of the study, without which we might have expected some of the more recently opened cases to have started earlier and therefore to have appeared in the 'closed' column.

Direct work: problem definition

As has already been explained, the initial forum for defining the problems that were to be tackled was the series of meeting following referral. It is difficult, as usual in this context, to separate a statement of the problems in each case from the recommended intervention - especially as there was no opportunity for observation of the referral processes and hence for an independent measure, however imperfect, of the difficulties experienced by the clients.

Accordingly no attempt will be made to present and artificial distinction between 'real' problems and those perceived to be amenable to intervention. The purpose of this section is to give the reader a flavour of what kinds of issues the Project took up in its direct work with clients. This is best achieved by a simple listing of the problems and objectives as defined at the initial stages. Quotation marks in the following indicate that the interviews with M.A.R.S. staff are being cited. (Fuller accounts of some of these cases are to be found in Appendix 1.)

The Chatfield family

The family was referred by the hospital social worker in consultation with the child psychiatrist. Mrs Chatfield, a lone parent, was having difficulty in controlling her two children, aged 8 and 10, especially the eldest who had been admitted to hospital after taking bleach. The mother was believed to need help in parenting skills, of a practical kind for which conventional sessions with the psychiatrist were proving ineffective and inappropriate. The M.A.R.S. objective was to work directly with the mother, in conjunction with the social worker, to help her learn better ways of handling the children.

39

Sammy Murdoch

Sammy, aged 15, was referred by the educational psychologist. He had little or no experience of ordinary schooling, and plans to place him in a List G school had not materialised. After a lengthy period in the assessment centre, he was returned home to his lone mother, and the M.A.R.S. referral was part of a package whereby 1:1 teaching sessions at the Project premises would be supported by individual work with Sammy designed to offer him a 'good experience' with a male worker, some social skills, and an 'outlet', in order to protect his mother from the aggressiveness which, it was expected, would build up during the teaching time. Support was also to be offered, if necessary, to the 1:1 teacher. This was a measure expected to last only until Sammy reached the statutory school-leaving age.

Peter Bryant

Peter was referred by his social worker following numerous offences and lengthy non-attendance at school. There was thought to be the strong possibility of a List D placement. The intention was to reintegrate him gradually into mainstream education by building up his attendance, initially by a 1:1 arrangement. The M.A.R.S. objective was to provide support to this plan by offering a 'consistent adult involvement' which it was felt he had hitherto lacked, and by encouraging him practically to attend the 1:1 sessions and eventually the school.

The Graham family

The family was referred by their social worker in consultation with a psychiatrist. The three children (of whom the eldest, a girl aged 8, was the one overtly referred) lived with Mrs Graham and her cohabitee. There had been difficult behaviour at both home and school, with the eldest girl stealing money from her mother; relationship problems between the mother and her cohabitee were causing concern about the children, and there had been past accusations of abuse. The social worker felt that the family would benefit from more intensive help than she had the time to provide, and the M.A.R.S. objectives were to investigate 'the ways in which Mrs Graham operated with her children ... and to suggest to her ways of how to control and improve their behaviour'.

Jimmy Shaw

Jimmy, aged 15, was referred by his school with the agreement of his social worker, after his discharge from a List D school, to which he had gone following offences. On his return to his parents in Dundee, the improvements in his self-image and ability to mix with peers which were said to have taken place in the residential setting were being eroded by a failure to get him swiftly reintegrated into a mainstream school. (The failure was said to result from both bureaucratic delays and Jimmy's extreme reluctance.) There was concern lest he should fail to attend and re-offend. The social worker was not able to give the case much priority, and the M.A.R.S. objective was to help 'create a routine' for Jimmy to attend 1:1 sessions and eventually to reintegrate fully into schooling.

Alan Hawkins

Alan was referred at the age of 12 by his educational social worker as part of a very explicitly worked out package. He was due to go to a List G school in six months time, after manifesting serious behaviour problems and being excluded from school in Dundee. At home he had been the focus of disputes and rivalry between his mother and her cohabitee, and the concern was that the List G placement might be overtaken by a domestic crisis and/or that it might break down. The M.A.R.S. objective was to ease the transition by working ion his reputedly unmanageable behaviour and to prepare him for the group living he would experience in the residential school placement.

Wayne Clark

Wayne, a seven year old, was referred by his social worker. Despite his youth he had a considerable reputation at school and in the local community for unmanageable behaviour, and had committed numerous offences. He was said to be beyond the control of his mother, who had recently separated from his father. There was a clear risk of his being admitted to care. The M.A.R.S. objective was to work with the mother to 'get some living routine' around the care of Wayne outside school hours, and to devise a behaviour modification programme for him at school.

Mrs Mansfield

A lone mother of five children, Mrs Mansfield was referred by the educational social worker. The children, some of whom were mentally or physically handicapped, had experienced a variety of attendance problems and in-care episodes. The referral was not triggered by any particular incident, but was in the nature of a last resort. The social worker was concerned about the general standard of care in the family, and in particular by the mother's tendency to mistrust professional help. The M.A.R.S. objective was to try to 'alter the dynamics' of the family by working with the mother, in the hope that she might be persuaded to 'release' the children and permit them to receive preferable forms of professional help.

Donald Mulligan

Donald, aged 14, was referred by his social worker, shortly after his arrival at a children's home in Dundee. He was refusing to go to school, and was presenting management problems in the home, having spent most of hhis life in care and had several recent changes of placement. A complicating factor was a disagreement within the social work department about the nature and seriousness of his problems, and the resultant absence of a long-term plan. The M.A.R.S. objective was to undertake life-history work with Donald to enhance his own understanding of his present position, and to promote the formation of a plan by helping to improve communications between the different professional parties involved.

Simon Dent

Simon, aged 15, was referred by his social worker after his removal from a children's home to the assessment centre. He came from a family described as 'chaotic and volatile', had longstanding attendance problems, and there was a suspicion that he had become involved in homosexual prostitution while at the children's home (not on the premises). The M.A.R.S. objective was to form a personal relationship with him as a means of 'improving his sense of self worth' and subsequently to discuss with him issues of sexuality and risk.

Lucy Miller

Lucy was referred by her social worker at the age of 11, at a time when concern was being expressed by the school about her behaviour, which included stealing on the premises and at lunchtime, and fighting. Lucy and her younger siblings were on the child protection register, and the family had been referred to the psychiatrist. Although this was referred to as a 'family' case, it was felt that Lucy needed individual work, and the

M.A.R.S. objective was to 'attempt to engage with her', and involve her in constructive activities, with family work being a subsequent option.

Stuart Jeavons

Stuart, aged 15, was referred by his school in conjunction with his social worker. He had been excluded from school following disruptive behaviour and regular truanting, which had deteriorated following his return home after a recent period in residential care. The M.A.R.S. objective was short term: to engage him in constructive community activities, and to help establish a regular attendance pattern with the 1:1 teacher that was being sought for him.

Theory and practice

A more systematic and codified account of these objectives can be found in Chapter 6. Meanwhile some comments can be made on the extent to which they reflect the general M.A.R.S. approach as set out in earlier chapters.

Only one of the cases, that of Donald Mulligan, seems to exemplify **prominently** the aspirations of the Project to promote the resolution of problems of communication or cooperation between professionals. In other cases this element was less to the forefront, and figured usually in suggestions that the M.A.R.S. presence could speed up or tighten the coordination required in devising and implementing 1:1 packages where there was involvement of both social work and educational departments.

In fact, though, this is to underestimate the day-to-day concerns of Project staff with the manner in which statutory sector professionals were operating in these cases. In most of them, part of the original contract incorporated an agreed division of labour between referrers and Project staff. In the case of the Chatfields, for example, the hospital social worker was supposed to develop a counselling relationship with the mother, while the M.A.R.S. role was to be a more 'practical' one. Whatever the (perhaps precarious) standing of this distinction, however, the allocation of roles did not work as the case developed because the social worker was unable to devote enough time to the case. Similar patterns developed in other cases, and the M.A.R.S. staff would frequently be devoting time and effort to encouraging the statutory workers fulfil (as M.A.R.S. workers saw it) their undertakings. This was a contentious issue in the relationship between M.A.R.S. and the statutory sector and is further discussed, from the perspective of the statutory workers, in Chapter 8.

Returning to the description of problems and objectives, these could be grouped in various other ways. One distinction is between those cases where the M.A.R.S. role was part of a strategy, usually an educational package, where a distinct and seemingly customary model was being followed (for example Peter Bryant) and those on the other hand where the Project staff were more involved in making the rules anew to suit a particular set of problems, as with the Chatfields. A second distinction is between those where the commitment was open-ended The Chatfields, again) those where it was time-limited by some factor or other (Sammy Murdoch's school-leaving date); overlapping but not identical is the difference between cases where the objectives were provisional only (Donald Mulligan), subject to refinement or modification, and where they were, at least in intention, definitive (Mrs Mansfield). Fourthly, the objectives may differ in emphasis according to whether the hoped-for changes were expressed in terms of personal functioning (Mrs Mansfield) or as some form of service target, such as achieving school attendance or avoiding entry to care (Jimmy Shaw).

These distinctions are obviously tentative and fluid, and their interest does not lie in any conclusions about their respective incidence but rather in the light they shed on the Project's working concepts and methods. Interesting questions arise about this. Does the range and heterogeneity of problems taken up, objectives set, and scope and variety of work undertaken indicate a valuable degree of flexibility? Or are these features evidence of looseness in the formulation of Project policy, of a potential for drift in the controlling definitions of what M.A.R.S. can and cannot address? Or, at a less overt level, do these apparent differences in the kinds of work taken on mask an underlying coherence or even sameness of method - whether appropriate or not? These questions, to which there is no easy answer, need to be considered in the light of data reported in subsequent pages. We now turn in the next chapter to a more detailed look at the working methods and processes of the Project.

5 Preventive work in practice

Social work research sets itself an extremely difficult challenge if it aspires to link outcomes with the processes of intervention. It is one thing to be able to say that intervention has produced, or more likely appears to have produced, a particular effect, but quite another to explain how precisely this has come about. In lieu of a utopian research design which would establish such causal links (see Chapter 7), the purpose of this chapter is to offer a careful description of the Projects processes and working methods with its clients. This is partly with the intention of providing the reader the material on which to base a judgment of how the Project achieved the results it did, and partly for its interest in its own right. Data from the observation of a number of working sessions will be reported; it is introduced and set in context by drawing further on the group interviews with staff.

Working methods: the staff view

I think what we do is really just thoughtful, caring, good-quality social work ... it's dangerous in the sense that it's entirely our interpretation...

An attempt was made to cross-examine this brave statement from the Project leader. What, in the context in which M.A.R.S. operates, is 'thoughtful ... social work'? Among the terms used by Project staff to describe the repertoire of working methods were 'informal activity-based work', 'counselling', 'family therapy or family work', and 'behaviour modification' - a list which reveals a similar eclecticism to that which was noted in Chapter 3 at the level of theory. The most notable absentee from this repertoire of methods is probably groupwork, an omission which may seem critical to some since several of the children's difficulties (in mixing with peers for example) were those for which groupwork techniques are usually held to be appropriate. It is, however, difficult to see how groups could have been organised with the small numbers dealt with by the Project, though staff were often engaged in encouraging children to attend groups run by other agencies such as the IT centre.

One particular point was pursued that will throw some light on the ensuing accounts of the sessions observed. It had been noted that in direct work cases the division of responsibility between M.A.R.S. and the statutory social worker was often described in terms of the relative formality of the social worker's relationship with the client and the relative informality of the M.A.R.S. worker's. This was explained as growing naturally out of the social worker's 'official' role, possibly with statutory responsibility to discharge in the form of an order, but in any case having in the eyes of the client official accountability. The M.A.R.S. worker was therefore better placed to form a friendly and more relaxed relationship with the client.

This informality, however, was seen as being accompanied by an underlying professional strategy, perhaps in a 'covert' way (a term, unfashionably but probably honestly, in quite frequent use in the Project). When pressed, in the context of an individual case where the nature and focus of intervention had altered several times, to distinguish between 'informality', a counselling role, and 'therapy', staff had some difficulty, at least with the first two terms:

> counselling is giving advice, before we were just chatting, gossiping ... I'm finding it hard to separate them out. Therapy, yes, I can identify therapy, but in terms of counselling, advice, activity ... in fact you wrap up what can be a social worker's sense sitting across a desk and talking with somebody, we've that wrapped up into getting involved with somebody in an informal, chatty activity, whatever. The therapy ... that we set up deliberately, with two people, tape-recorder, the video, or going into the other room, that's very clearly separate. With the rest of it I would say we wrap up all the social work skills in what is apparently a very informal setting.

46

A cynical response might be that this has elements of both preciosity and an apologia for some rather meaningless and undisciplined 'relationship work' of the kind for which social workers are often criticised. The M.A.R.S. staff were well aware of such a view. When asked whether the informality, and all that it implied, was difficult to reconcile with the sophistication which they sought to bring to bear on casework, a staff member was concerned to stress that their unstructured style of working makes particular demands precisely on the worker's professional skills and self-discipline: 'to play a role like that you almost have to be more aware of what you're doing ... trying to be consistent is more difficult.'

There were further elements in the relaxed nature of some aspects of direct work. An informal approach was used, quite straightforwardly and explicitly, as a means of building up an initial relationship with children who had often been, in the view of Project staff, subjected to constant pressure when in contact with other professionals and with adults generally. Creating a relationship of trust with a caring adult was often seen first as a professional end in itself, an experience for clients of some form of good parenting; and secondly as a means to other ends which required this foundation, if for example more intensive professional input was to follow, or if the client needed to be persuaded to accept the intervention of other agencies. Similarly, the Project would often aim explicitly to provide quite simply an enjoyable time for clients whose lives might not be overflowing with such opportunities.

This glance at some of the Project's working methods in direct work cases did not of course exhaust their repertoire, but serves to lead into a discussion of the observation data.

Direct work observed

Direct work was observed with three clients, each on three separate occasions: a total of nine two-hour sessions. The sessions had to be chosen in part on pragmatic grounds, on the basis of which cases were of a kind which would not in the judgement of staff be disturbed by an outsider's presence, which clients would give their consent, and which were available at a particular time. A range of the Project's working style was included, but the more intensive or 'therapeutic' kinds of client contact were under-represented. The clients concerned were one family, and two individual children, a boy and a girl. One had been an active case for some 15 months, one for a few months, and one for a few weeks only. It is probable, of course, that the participation of a researcher had some inhibiting impact on the nature of the sessions, and the adult client, at least, might have been unlikely to have raised any very difficult personal issues in his presence. On subsequent discussion with the workers this did not seem to have been a major factor in the particular sessions chosen, and in fact two of the clients had already been met and interviewed for the study.

The method used was to divide up the sessions into ten-minute periods, and, where conditions permitted, to make on-the-spot notes of proceedings in two columns, one of 'activities' and 'staff-client interaction'. The sessions were discussed afterwards with M.A.R.S. staff.

The observation was designed to go a little beyond simple description, though that was seen as important. The sessions were observed to include two broad types of interaction. For a significant proportion of the time, it would have been difficult, without prior knowledge, to guess that the transactions were those of social worker(s) and client(s). This sort of interaction, similar to what might take place on any social occasion involving a similar group of people, was labelled (not altogether satisfactorily) 'casual'. The second type of interaction appeared to bear more overtly the mark of the actual professional context of the occasion, and was characterised as 'structured'. This is a hazardous distinction in view of the points made above, especially those concerning the wider professional uses of informality, and the analysis tries to take account of any 'covert' professional content. The rough twofold analysis that resulted is not an attempt to assess the **amount** of purposeful talk, since the M.A.R.S. strategy of planned informality would suggest that all or at least most of the interaction, including the 'casual', was purposeful. It is rather an attempt to document the balance between the overtly different kinds of interaction taking place, and to provide material for the reader to judge the purposefulness of the sessions. The results of the exercise are now reported session by session for each client, with some brief preceding explanation of the context and added comment.

The Chatfield family

Brief details of the background of Mrs Chatfield, Kim and Arthur are given in Chapter 4 and in Appendix 1. Originally, the intervention with the family had been in the form of a single session with everyone, preparing and cooking a meal in the Project kitchen, and being used to suggest practical ways for the lone parent Mrs Chatfield to fulfil her role as mother, particularly with regard to setting boundaries to the children's unruly behaviour. By the time of the observation, however, the M.A.R.S. role had developed considerably. The emphasis had become less practical, and more 'therapeutic', partly because the practical objectives were seen as having been at least partially achieved, partly because the statutory social worker had been unable to fulfil her agreed counselling role owing to competing priorities, and partly, it seemed, spontaneously. A particular sequence of events had produced a domestic crisis and led to a closer and more personal relationship between Mrs Chatfield and the Project staff, and after considerable internal discussion it had been decided to 'change gear'.

The family were now having three sessions a week. One of these was the evening meal, which continued throughout. In addition Mrs Chatfield was now having a session on her own of 'personal work' designed to explore her life history and past problematic relationships, their effect on her self-image, and her hypothesised scapegoating of Kim. Kim was also having a personal session, activity-based but giving her the opportunity to 'process her feelings'. The sessions observed were the family mealtimes, whose purpose was now said to be to reinforce the earlier family work, to monitor developments in the family during the week, and generally to preserve the continuity of the family orientation. Two staff members from M.A.R.S. were involved in the sessions. Since the whole group was not always in the same room not all interaction could be observed.

Session one (4pm-6pm). The family did not arrive until 4.25. After initial welcome and showing of holiday photographs, the group divided, one worker going into the kitchen with Mrs Chatfield to finish the meal preparations (previously begun), while the other worker took the children into the sitting room to play a board game. After about 20 minutes, the group had their meal, lasting about 50 minutes. The rest of the session was occupied by washing up and putting away, with the children again playing a game, but helping finally in the clearing up.

The **interaction** was mostly classified as 'casual', with the family eager to talk about their recent holiday (Barnardo's-assisted). The following items were classified as 'structured'. There was some unobtrusive drawing out of the holiday experiences by the M.A.R.S. staff. On two occasions during the meal, Arthur was reprimanded over his table manners, once by each M.A.R.S. worker. The male worker seemed to be the one who organised the practical tasks (washing up and so on), determining who did what with acknowledged authority. He also took the lead after the meal in teaching various ways of playing the board game. In the kitchen after the meal, a private conversation between the other worker and Mrs Chatfield, initiated by the worker, sought to explore some of Kim's remarks about her holiday boyfriend and how the mother saw this.

Session two (4pm-6pm). A week later, this session followed a similar pattern. The family arrived at 4.20, and meal preliminaries lasted rather longer (50 minutes). During this there was cooking, a variety of conversations, board games, and a M.A.R.S. worker helping Arthur with a model car he was making, with much movement between three different rooms. The meal took half an hour, and clearing up 20 minutes.

The **interaction** seemed 'casual', to perhaps a greater degree than on the first occasion, with less drawing out. Mrs Chatfield initiated a discussion in the kitchen before the meal of Kim's school report, Kim being present and not apparently worried. This topic was taken up at intervals throughout the session. The instruction with the model car was probably to be classified as a planned input; otherwise there seemed little that was overtly structured.

Session three. This session, a week later still, was different in that one of the workers was unable to be present and the remaining worker went out with the family to a restaurant. This was paid for, like the food for the other meals, by the Project. The social experience itself (though this was not the first such visit) was the dominating influence on the occasion, conversation being mostly 'casual' with an element of reprimanding the children for mildly inappropriate behaviour as before.

Comment. It must be remembered that the family meal was by now a longstanding institution for both family and workers. The basic structure of the sessions had obvious taken for granted features on both sides, and the M.A.R.S. staff were seamlessly following established routines, which included their predominantly avuncular (or auntly?), slightly pedagogic tone with the children. The session was clearly a pleasantly special experience for a severely deprived family, and provided an opportunity for the preservation of Mrs Chatfield's morale (said to be still precarious despite progress) and for the reinforcement of various social skills. The workers noted some reaction from Mrs Chatfield against their own quasi-parental behaviour towards the children (the reprimanding), and were speculating that this might be a positive development. This having been said, the proportion of the interaction classified as 'structured' was lower than might have been expected. Apart from the discussion of Kim's school report, there was little evidence of the monitoring of weekly developments said to have been one of the purposes.

The informality cited earlier was certainly demonstrated. The regular case reviews within the Project had expressed concern about the open-endedness of the work with this family: no natural end-point seemed in view. In particular, with the focus having shifted towards the more therapeutic individual sessions, the point of the continuing family sessions could be called into question, apart from their obvious function in providing something for the otherwise excluded Arthur. The extent to which insights from the family sessions fed into the individual sessions was difficult to pin down. It may be that the morale-preserving function of the occasions was sufficiently important to warrant their continuation, or that the observation failed to detect other aspects of their interaction.

Donald Mulligan

Brief details of the background are again to be found in Chapter 4 and Appendix 1. Donald (aged 14) had been in care most of his life, and his current placement in a children's home had been precarious owing to his recalcitrant behaviour and refusal to attend school; no plan had yet been formed for his future. The M.A.R.S. contribution to the overall management of his case was partly designed to resolve confusions within the social work department, but the objectives of the individual sessions with Donald were to construct a life story, and to use it as the basis for discussing with him the way decisions had in the past been made about him and how they might be made about his future. At the time of the observation, the life story work had been partially completed and the discussions were ongoing, being developed around practical activities. Donald had learnt things about his earlier life, especially about the circumstances in which he entered care as a baby, which surprised and puzzled him, and negotiations were in hand for him to have sight of his social work file. He had been found to be a more articulate boy than expected. Meanwhile his position at the home was slightly less precarious, but arrangements needed to be made about his schooling. Only one member of staff was involved in this case.

Session one (12.30pm-2.30pm). Donald arrived slightly late, and the first 40 minutes were occupied with a snack lunch. Conversation continued at the table and while washing up. Ten minutes were then spent planning practical activities (the making of a table). After another member of staff was called in to advise, they made decisions about timber to be bought, and spent the remainder of the session on a trip to a timber warehouse to make the purchases. This was on foot and took one hour.

The **interaction** during the first hour was a mixture of 'casual' (in this case practical) and 'structured' personal talk. The former was led by the worker, who appeared deliberately to make it egalitarian - this helped by the fact that she was not herself an expert joiner. The personal talk was introduced at intervals, about evenly distributed, during lunch and clearing away. Topics included discoveries about Donald's family history, and his social worker and the arrangements for seeing his file. The M.A.R.S. worker had obtained a copy of his birth certificate, which she handed over. These conversations, lasting perhaps 20 minutes, seemed designed (successfully) to get Donald to think about and express his feelings towards his natural parents and siblings. This was not purely a historical issue for him, as he had recently made contact with his natural father and was spending periods of time with him.

Session two (10am-12 noon). This session was two months later, weekly sessions not having been maintained for various reasons, though some had taken place. Donald did not arrive until 10.30. The activity consisted of one hour's working on the table, planned the previous occasion: drilling, screwing parts together, and varnishing, interspersed with conversation, with the worker taking an equal part of the 'work'. The remaining half-hour was spent drinking coffee and playing computer games.

The **interaction** again consisted of a mixture, perhaps half and half during the first hour, of 'casual' activity-oriented talk and 'structured' personal talk. The latter was at least partly initiated by Donald, and included some clearly difficult areas: Donald's feelings about his father and brother, and their recent troubles with the police; also about a foster family he had spent time with in the past; about school attendance; and about his impending change of social worker. There was further talk, initiated by the worker, of the still unfinished life story book. The most overtly serious part of all this was the talk of Donald's natural family. The worker, who saw him as 'confused' in his feelings about them, used his raising of the topic to seek clarify his feelings, and to elicit a view from him about how much he wanted to see of them in the future. She was discouraging him from getting too precipitately involved, and quietly reinforced any tendency he expressed in the opposite direction.

Session three (10am-12 noon). This was a week later, and was spent entirely outdoors, overrunning by three quarters of an hour. A fishing expedition had been planned: Donald and the worker went to buy hooks, spent some time digging on the beach for bait, and fished in the sea. The worker had gone to some trouble to organise this, but, alas, no fish were caught.

The **interaction** was almost entirely casual, with two exceptions. There was discussion of Donald's planned trip to stay with his former foster-parents (later that day), with the worker asking for some family details for her own information, but also with an encouraging tone. She also told Donald of the report she had written for the Reporter to the Children's

Hearing, to whom Donald had been referred over his school attendance. She relayed what she had recommended, which included a 1:1 teacher, and they discussed this, and the time it might take to get an arrangement under way.

There was a postscript to this session. In fact Donald did not go to the foster family afterwards, but, much to the surprise of the worker, absconded to England and was missing for several days, some of them spent in the company of his natural father.

Comment. The overall client-centred objectives for this boy had been provisional only, with an assessment function: the M.A.R.S. worker was to form a relationship with him, talk to him about his early life, and help him think about his future and his own role in taking decisions about it. The confusions surrounding the case, both in Donald's own mind and among the professionals (see appendix 1) seemed to make these provisional targets appropriate. On the surface the use of informal activity-based sessions to build up a relationship of trust seemed to be successful in terms of the topics discussed in a 'structured' manner, though the sequel to the last session showed that the trust was not complete. The episode was interpreted by the M.A.R.S. staff as showing Donald, still unsure of adults, engaged in a normal process of testing out, and the sessions were not interrupted by it.

There were obviously hard questions ahead in this case. The stability of the existing placement was far from established, and the education aspects were yet to be handled; though a strategy was crystallising in the mind of the worker, the provisional objectives had not yet been formally superseded. Most important, perhaps, was the decision, presumably to be made on the basis of the kind of work observed, as to whether Donald would be able to accept the kind of help M.A.R.S. had to offer. Could this be one of those cases discussed in a previous chapter where 'damage' was too great for the M.A.R.S. style of work?

Lucy Miller

Lucy (aged 11) had been seriously troublesome at school, and it was suspected that family problems were contributing to this. The eldest in a family of four (all on the child protection register), Lucy seemed to have been treated differently from her siblings and was the only one whose behaviour was troublesome. The social worker had referred her in the expectation of tapping the Project's 'expertise in family work', but it was believed that, initially at least, Lucy needed individual work. The sessions observed took place very soon after the referral, the worker having met

Lucy on four occasions only. The objectives were again provisional, to engage with the child through activities and encourage her to talk about her stealing and, if judged appropriate, about the abuse she was thought to have experienced some years previously. The observation took place on three successive weeks during the Summer holidays.

Session one (2pm-4pm). The first session was outside the Project, mainly devoted to picking up litter on the beach as part of a scheme run by the council. Lucy was collected by car from her home, the opportunity being taken to talk for a few minutes with her parents, and driven to the beach. An hour was spent conscientiously picking up litter, and then half an hour in a local cafe before returning home.

The **interaction** was almost entirely 'casual' or lightly chatty, with no real differences in tone discernible. There was some talk of the 'drawing out' kind about school and family, but troublesome behaviour was not touched upon. There was discussion of making things (Lucy was frustrated by not having been able to finish off a number of things she had begun to make with her hands), and plans for future sessions were made.

Session two (2pm-4pm). Two sorts of practical activity had been planned. The worker brought Lucy to the Project by car, and 40 minutes were spent making a cake, with the worker giving instructions. While it was in the oven, they set to to cover a tupperware box with shells using Polyfilla. This not wholly successful effort occupied the rest of the session.

Once again the **interaction** was largely 'casual', a quite conventional kitchen scene. The worker spent quite a lot of time instructing Lucy in the two tasks, but encouraging her at the same time to find out things for herself. Lucy was absorbed in her work, and was also quite visibly enjoying herself. The worker complimented her on her patience, and suggested that this could be applied to other tasks.

Session three (2pm-4pm). The session was again spent in practical activities, the shell-box being varnished (it having been completed by the M.A.R.S. worker during the week), and the cake from the previous week being iced and decorated. A photograph was taken of the completed article. A sweater which Lucy had knitted, with help from the worker, was also displayed, proudly, to other staff in the Project.

The interaction seemed to include a somewhat higher proportion of 'structured' and significant talk than in previous sessions. There was a seemingly more deliberate attempt to draw Lucy into discussing her week's experiences. Her persistence in finishing the sweater was reinforced. The cake decoration was used as an opportunity to discuss how to get ideas by consulting books. The majority of the interaction was nevertheless of the 'casual' type. The Project secretary made a significant contribution to the session.

Comment. Of all the sessions observed, these were the least dense in overtly 'structured' input. Without knowledge of the background it would have been difficult to guess that the child had been referred to a social work agency. This in itself is perhaps a tribute to the worker's ability to create a natural atmosphere. Lucy was successfully 'engaged with', more so, reportedly than by other adults, and her natural aptitude for craft work brought out; the troublesome behaviour had not recurred, though schools were on holiday at the time. This behaviour, however, was never referred to during the sessions, though it had been during an earlier (unobserved) one.

The purposefulness of this work could only be judged after the event, that is after the end of the study fieldwork. Plans for working with the parents were still under consideration at this time, and attempts were being made when Lucy was picked up to 'engage' in some sense with them also. There was however a difficulty in the absence of any statutory order which, it was thought, would provide a way into family work.

This illustrates a general difficulty which M.A.R.S. rather struggled to resolve. Working with the child rather than the family as a whole was frankly admitted to be an easy option:

> I would say generally I wouldn't opt to work with a family, I would take the easiest course first. If you're going to work with the whole family, you're into open-ended limitless work...

It was added that they would normally hope that the social worker would have a relationship with parents that could be part of a concerted strategy. Evidently this had not, or not yet, been developed in the case of the Millers.

It is important to comment further on the significance of the observation data for the study. As has been noted the working processes documented are unlikely to have been representative of the totality of the M.A.R.S. methods, even of those in direct work cases: the more 'intense' types of client contact are under-represented, and work with the staff of other agencies is not covered at all. Although, it is hoped, a flavour is given of a significant proportion of the M.A.R.S. style of working and of the skills involved, a dominant impression may well have been given of greater degree of relaxation and freedom from pressure than was typically the case. This would apply particularly to the case of the Chatfields, an involvement of long standing.

A longer period of observation would not have been feasible in this study, and there must be doubts as to whether it would be feasible in many studies, given the extreme labour-intensiveness of the research method. England (1987) has suggested that only a quasi-literary approach, where work on a case is analysed in the kind of detail and with the kind of stance used in the critical appreciation of a work of literature, can do justice to the intuitive and inescapably 'subjective' dimensions of social work. This is seductive, and the subject warrants longer treatment than it can be given here (see Smith, 1987), but there would seem to be serious logistical problems (among others discussed by Smith) in applying it in most research circumstances.

The next chapter explores the effectiveness of the work documented here.

6 Goals and achievements

There were two possible approaches to the question of effectiveness. Since this study was conceived as an analysis of preventive work (if of a particular kind) one possibility was to use an *a priori* definition of the preventive goals, and seek to ascertain whether these had been achieved. The risk with this approach is that although the Project defined itself as 'preventive', this kind of self-definition could have been at such a level of abstraction that the goal might have borne little relation to working practices. In other words, the goals may be subtly distorted if the analyst tries to fit them into some pre-ordained preventive mould. An alternative possibility was to confine the analysis to the objectives actually set in individual cases, whether or not they could reasonably be classed as preventive, and to draw conclusion about the effectiveness of the work in this looser and less standardisable way.

In fact a combination of both these approaches was used in the study. Preventive objectives were standardised up to a certain point, after discussion which sought to ground them in the reality of the M.A.R.S. context. Individual cases were then classified according to which objectives from the resulting fixed choice list were being pursued, giving a measure of the more common types of goal being addressed by the Project. The next step was to assess with Project staff, using a ranking procedure, the extent to which individual goals had been met. The results of this were compared with responses given in interviews with referrers and with those clients who agreed to be interviewed. Since the clarification of preventive objectives is itself of substantive interest, an account will be given of how the basic categorisation of objectives was arrived at.

Preventive objectives

An initial typology of seven preventive goals was suggested by Holman's (1988) study of preventive work in the voluntary sector. This seven-fold categorisation was discussed with the M.A.R.S. staff as a starting point for the development of a list of preventive objectives applicable to their own work. Holman's list was as follows:

1. prevention of entry into care or separation from natural family;

2. prevention of entry into custodial care;

3. prevention of neglect or abuse of children by improving parenting capacities;

4. preventing the harmful effects of poor parenting;

5. prevention of disadvantage in homes or communities;

6. prevention (once children are separated) of long stays away from home by rehabilitation;

7. prevention (once children are separated) of isolation in care.

When staff were asked in general terms (i.e. without reference to individual cases) how far this list reflected their own objectives, a number of modifications was suggested. It was thought that item 5, with its community work flavour, was in general not applicable to M.A.R.S. Items 3 and 4 were found hard to distinguish, and it was agreed that clarity would be improved if 'other' was used to qualify 'harmful effects' in item 4. Some additional categories were argued for, reflecting in part the relationship of the Project to the statutory sector: 'prevention of rejection by other professional staff', and 'prevention of professional muddle or lack of planning' were added to the list. It was also decided to add two more behavioural goals, which after discussion were characterised as 'preventing the deterioration of children's behaviour' and 'preventing the deterioration of family relationships'. The last two additions have the technical disadvantage, which research-minded readers will have noticed, of increasing the possibilities which were already present of the goals not being mutually exclusive.

Table 6.1
Preventive goals

		ranked 1st	all
1.	Entry into care	1	5
2.	Entry into custodial care	1	2
3.	Neglect or abuse of children	2	2
4.	Other harmful effects (parenting)	1	5
5.	Disadvantage (homes/communities)	-	1
6.	Long stays in care	-	1
7.	Isolation in care	1	1
8.	Rejection by professionals	3	4
9.	'Professional muddle'	-	6
10.	Behavioural - child	2	6
11.	Behavioural - family	-	3
12.	Other*	1	8

* 'other' included mainly educational objectives

With the list revised in this way (see Table 6.1), but the discussion continuing in general terms, the commonest overall goal was believed to be the prevention of rejection, followed by items 3 and 4 from the original list. The least common were believed to be items 2 and 7, followed by item 7. This, perhaps, is evidence of little more than the mental set of Project staff at the time at which the exercise was carried out. Did the identification of goals by individual case reveal any differences?

For this the staff were asked to identify objectives for each case in the direct work sample, without restriction as to number in each case; they were also asked to rank them in order of priority. The results appear in Table 6.1, with the goal ranked as first priority being included separately.

The first thing to note is the range of the objectives in individual cases. This underlines (if need be) the difficulties of treating 'preventive work' as a single category, and serves to remind us of the hazards of seeking to evaluate its effectiveness. It also emphasises the multiplicity of objectives within cases, with an average of 3.7 goals per case being identified: a further problem for the evaluator. These findings prompt some reflection back on the expressed overall aim of M.A.R.S. to work in cases where a crisis of some sort was creating an imminent risk of breakdown. If this had been the most common scenario, one might have expected that item 1 would have loomed larger than it does among first priorities, and even larger than it does among all priorities.

There are various ways in which the range of different objectives could be grouped, each inevitably involving loss of distinctions and awkward bedfellows. It was decided, however, for ease of analysis and scanning, to combine categories in subsequent presentation of the data. The composite categories are 'objectives associated with the care system' (items 1,2,6,7), 'parenting objectives' (items 3,4), 'behavioural objectives' (items 10,11), 'professional objectives' (items 8,9) and 'other' (items 5,12).

Staff were asked to rate on a four-point scale the success of their intervention on each of the first three objectives in each case. The points of the scale were 'completely successful', 'partially successful', 'rather unsuccessful', and 'completely unsuccessful'. An obvious problem in doing this arose from the different stages that the cases had reached. Since it is probably misleading to regard each intervention period as following a coherent sequence of beginning, middle, and end (we have seen how objectives can change and develop over time), it was thought justifiable to take a standard slice of life in the clients' time with M.A.R.S. Staff were therefore asked to consider the last six months, either in the sense of immediately preceding the rating point, for cases still open, or for closed cases the final six months. Staff were also given the option of indicating a 'don't know, or too soon to tell', which was only used once.

The results of the rating of the goal ranked as first priority are shown in Table 6.2.

Table 6.2
Success rating for first objective

	completely suc'l	partially suc'l	rather unsuc'l	completely unsuc'l	d/k
care system	2	-	-	1	-
parenting	-	2	-	1	-
behavioural	1	-	1	-	-
professional	2	1	-	-	-
other	1	-	-	-	-
total	6	3	1	2	-

Overall (rated by the staff themselves it should be remembered) the first priority had been achieved in nine out of twelve cases. Little can be made of the distribution of these figures between the different categories. If, however, we include all of the first three objectives for each case, and in addition collapse the successful and unsuccessful categories, then something of a pattern emerges (Table 6.3).

The overall success rate is not greatly altered by including three objectives rather than one. The pattern suggested, however, is that the improvement of parenting capacities was more elusive of success than the other groups of objectives. This must of course be treated with caution. Quite apart from the small sample size, there was no test of the reliability of the categories (especially when collapsed), and no attempt to weight the individual objectives for seriousness, difficulty, or inter-relatedness within a case. Nevertheless the finding has a certain face validity. The Project had easier access to children and to professionals in the care system than to parents (cf the case of Lucy Miller), and there are good grounds for thinking that even if this were not the case, influencing parenting or family behaviour is simply more difficult, especially in an agency geared primarily towards individual working.

Table 6.3
Success rating for first three objectives

	successful	unsuccessful	d/k
care system	5	1	-
parenting	2	4	1
behavioural	4	1	-
professional	9	-	-
other	5	-	-
total	25	6	1

NB   The totals add up to less than 36 because fewer than three objectives were identified in some cases.

It has been stressed that the ratings on which the foregoing discussion is based were carried out by M.A.R.S. staff. We now turn to the perspectives of other parties involved.

Effectiveness as seen by clients and referrers

It may be regretted that the same rating instrument was not used with clients and referrers, so that their assessments might be compared directly with those of the M.A.R.S. staff. The reason for this was that these interviews were carried out as an exercise in pluralistic evaluation (Smith and Cantley 1984), the rationale for which is that different parties are likely to have different objectives. This would imply going through a wholly independent objective-defining stage, a procedure considered too cumbersome for the scale of the study and the patience of the respondents. As we shall see the assumption on which this decision was based was not fully borne out. As it is, the views of clients and of social work referrers remained in the form of responses to open-ended questions.

Clients were contacted by letter and their permission for an interview sought. Five parents declined or failed to reply after a reminder. The client perspective is therefore available in seven cases only, with six parents or couples and three of the older children being interviewed. They were asked about their experiences of going to M.A.R.S. and being with the Project, the differences between M.A.R.S. and other agencies, and their view of the effects for them (see appendix 1). In general the clients expressed views that were extremely favourable towards the Project and were outspoken in their regard for the staff as individuals. As has been found in other client research (e.g. Glendinning, 1986), the warmth of this regard seemed more important to them than the questions asked concerning specific ways in which they might have benefited from the contact.

The social workers of nine of the sample were interviewed. They were as would be expected more mixed in their views about the Project, as will be seen in Chapter 8. Here we concentrate on those aspects of the interview which deal with the objectives of the referral and the perceived effectiveness of the intervention.

To deal first with the definition of specific objectives: comparing the social workers and the M.A.R.S. staff, there was a considerable degree of congruence. To a certain extent this was to be expected, since each would have had a copy of the minutes of the meetings at which objectives had been agreed, but there was no evidence of different interpretations having developed or of lingering ambiguities. (This leaves open of course the different question of larger views about the function of the Project: reasons for making the initial referral might be different from objectives identified and agreed once the referral has been made.) Such differences as there were were those of emphasis, with M.A.R.S. workers being somewhat more specific about the personal work, or else reflected a particular departmental perspective. One social worker, for example, describing a case where the M.A.R.S. role was to provide support to an educational package, added the rider that an additional purpose was to reduce anxiety among the professionals about school attendance through the presence of the Project.

The clients' views on objectives were more difficult to align with those of the M.A.R.S. staff. Again, this was to be expected. Not only the word 'objective' itself (which was avoided in the interviews), but also, perhaps, the idea of having an objective seemed to come less readily to the minds of clients who were not completely voluntary in their involvement and who had experienced much previous contact with different agencies. While there was no evidence of clients seeing purposes that contradicted those of the professionals - usually translated into more demotic language - there were additional aims in the minds of the latter which the clients were either unaware of or not willing to confide to an interviewer. These were generally cases where parents saw the intervention in terms of children's behaviour, when there were concerns on the part of M.A.R.S. and social workers that this behaviour was related to family dynamics. The fact that fewer parents than professionals advanced family-centred reasons for the involvement is perhaps not very remarkable.

The general Project objective of investing a great deal in clarifying goals seemed then to have been largely successful in these cases. In giving their responses to questions about effectiveness, clients and social workers were working on a basis of broad agreement about aims.

In their assessment of the effects of the Project's intervention, the **social workers'** views were in general agreement with those of the M.A.R.S. workers. This was so both at the planning level (the identification of the appropriate strategy), and at that of the intensive work. There were no instances of social workers giving less favourable verdicts than the Project staff.

In one or two cases, doubts were expressed about the degree to which M.A.R.S. staff were fully aware of differences in the way clients presented themselves to the Project and the way they behaved outside it. It was stated in two cases, for example that '[Sammy Murdoch] enjoyed the personal attention and looked forward to it, there were no problems about his behaviour at M.A.R.S., but I couldn't see much evidence of it carrying over outside the sessions'; and 'Mrs Chatfield feels responsible for her actions when [M.A.R.S. staff] are around and would find it difficult to admit to failure or problems to them - she's more likely to to me'. Although this kind of point - each offered as a reservation only within an assessment that was favourable overall - does not necessarily appear in the Project's ratings above, examination of the interview transcripts shows that Project staff were aware of it. This remains something of a question mark, however - as is perhaps illustrated in the case of Donald Mulligan. The general question of 'carry-over' is a crucial one which is difficult to cover adequately.

In at least one case the view of the social worker was **more** favourable than that of the M.A.R.S. worker. The first objective with Peter Bryant had been to avoid entry to care, with subsidiary objectives related to his behaviour and the family functioning; in fact Peter was admitted to a List D school, and this was classified in the Project as a failure. The view of the social worker was that the admission had been established as unavoidable, but that the presence of an independent worker had helped to convince the family of this. In answer to a question about how things might have gone without the M.A.R.S. involvement, the social worker replied that 'the admission would have been earlier, and would have happened with a less clear picture of the damaging nature of the family dynamics'; as it was conditions were created for work after admission to be more constructive. He was less explicit about how exactly this had come about, but the example was the clearest in the sample of positive results being seen as the outcome of **concerted** work between a statutory worker and M.A.R.S., as opposed to work carried out semi-independently by the Project. If as suggested the eventual admission was both inevitable and took place in a more planned and less crisis-driven context, then this could be represented as a successful piece of preventive work (compare the example quoted at the end of this chapter).

As implied above the clients' views were not expressed in so convenient a form for comparison, since for them the 'objectives' followed less clearly the conventional formulae of social work - and of research. Responses to questions about how they had benefited from being with M.A.R.S. included:

Mrs Chatfield	They helped a lot with the bairns, they've grown up and are more polite - other people have noticed...
Mr Miller	Lucy is making far superior progress, it's boosted her morale, making things and learning things, we've had no more trouble with the school...
Mrs Murdoch	Disaster was averted ... they've helped Sammy and me live together, they're really smashing people ... They've treated him with sense and discipline, he's [worker] like a pro-father.
Donald Mulligan	They've helped me a lot, told how to think things out.
Sammy Murdoch	They tells us how not to have fights with Mum...

In general, clients were able to respond to a more pointed question about what might have happened if they had not gone to M.A.R.S. For example:

Donald Mulligan	I'd have ended up in Oakbank, I was near enough because I wasn't going to school, I was pretending I was but I wasn't...

Sammy Murdoch	I would probably still be in Burnside [assessment centre], I'd've felt terrible away from Mum and home...
Mrs Chatfield	I'd have given up probably. I was asking for the kids to be taken into care last year, I couldna cope ... I feel much more confident about being with them now.
Mr Miller	We'd have had lots of problems, Lucy would have been put out of school. Mind, I hope **they** don't let her down...

The picture emerging from the ratings of Project staff, that about three quarters of the problems taken on in this small sample were dealt with with complete or partial success, is not seriously disturbed by the views that were gathered of social workers or clients. The data presented in this chapter as a whole, 'soft' though most of it is, would suggest what seems a high degree of effectiveness.

Inevitably, however, questions remain. As some social workers were anxious to point out, one of the features of M.A.R.S. is that the workers were able to select the cases they took on, and might be assumed to concentrate on those in which they would expect to be effective. They also set their own objectives in those cases. In these circumstances, how successful is 'success'? A separate question relates to the lack of an independent indicator of what might have happened if there had been no referral to the Project. Granted that there was observed and agreed improvement in the problems experienced by clients, how can we sure that this did not come about by means other than the M.A.R.S. intervention? The exercise reported in the next chapter was designed to reduce the area of uncertainty on these issues.

Before that, however, and as a postscript to this chapter, brief examples are given of two cases where the difficulties of assessing effectiveness are particularly well illustrated.

Mrs Mansfield - a failure?

Mrs Mansfield, the mother of nine children with a range of problems including physical disability, learning difficulties, and poor school attendance, had long been known to education social workers. She was said to be a hypochondriac, was constantly in debt, and living conditions were described as 'filthy'. A root problem was identified as her persistent avoidance of attempts to provide help. Unusually, the M.A.R.S. intervention focused entirely on the mother, though the concern was for the children. The intention was to alter the dynamic whereby she kept the children around her so that they might be 'released' into some preferable form of professional help. The method was to take Mrs Mansfield out of the house for a regular lunchtime meal, in the hope that focusing attention on her rather than on the children, in a 'time out' spirit, might alter her attitudes.

Although initial signs were promising, this proved almost entirely abortive. In theory the contract lasted several weeks, but the lunchtime appointment was only kept twice. During these occasions a relationship of trust began to develop, but Mrs Mansfield's motivation faded and the case was abandoned. This was somewhat to the relief of the M.A.R.S. worker, who was finding it difficult to see the way forward. She felt that it had been worth trying, but that the power of the client's subculture was too great for any impact to be made; the case became something of an example in the Project of what to be wary of attempting. Mrs Mansfield's own retrospective view was that the occasions had been quite enjoyable but 'not all that important'.

This case was clearly in an important sense a failure, perhaps unsurprisingly in view of the difficulty and a certain vagueness in what had been attempted. However it could be seen as useful, in that it was said to have clarified the issues for the education social worker, and to have confirmed her department in the view that too much time should not be wasted in pursuing the previous strategy in the case.

Wayne Clark - shifting sands

This was a long and involved case which the account simplifies. Originally Wayne had been referred at the age of seven, as a notoriously uncontrollable child at school and in the community, who had committed many offences, though under age. The initial aims were to avoid entry into care ('outwith control'), and the method was to work with the mother to create some sense of routine and order in the home. However, the mother's relationship with the father became an issue, and the work expanded to helping the parents decide if they wanted to part. The mother left home, and Wayne's behaviour escalated. After a period with his father, he entered care.

The objectives were now redefined again. Individual work with Wayne was undertaken, in order to explain and reassure, and to preserve his self-esteem. Decisions were being made about the longer term, and Wayne was placed in a children's home outside Dundee. There were problems, not of Wayne's making, in this placement, and meanwhile the mother was keen to resume care. The latter issue had been the subject of intense discussion between M.A.R.S. and the social worker; the M.A.R.S. worker maintained contact with Wayne in the placement on the basis of fortnightly visits.

The original objective had clearly not been achieved. It would seem however that in the developing circumstances admission was not only unavoidable but also desirable. A M.A.R.S. worker commented

> I think by the time he came into care a lot of the work was done in relation to his long-term future that we would actually have been running about doing **now**, and much less effectively, because as soon as a kid comes into care there's a lack of pressure on the social work department to achieve things. And also it changes dramatically the parents' relationship with the department.

These extremely important points (cf the earlier remarks about Peter Bryant) were to some extent acknowledged by the social worker, who was also very complimentary about the quality of the work done by M.A.R.S. with Wayne **after** his admission to the children's home. This was despite the fact that there was some disagreement between M.A.R.S. and the social worker in their respective assessment of Mrs Clark's desire to resume care.

This illustrates very well the capacity of a case to undergo radical changes of understanding and focus as events overtake the initial assessment. It could not be said that that assessment was in any way faulty, nor that it would be sensible to treat it as a number of discrete episodes.

In the next chapter an alternative way of assessing effectiveness is described.

7 An experiment in prediction

What has been done so far is to document, in largely qualitative terms but supported by a simple rating exercise, the extent to which the Project met its stated aims in direct work cases, as seen by the parties involved. Despite there having been a (perhaps surprisingly) large measure of agreement about the meeting of the objectives, many will believe that this is not a sufficiently established finding without further evidence. The further data that was sought was through the 'prediction exercise', the rationale for which requires an extended discussion which returns to first principles.

The control group dilemma

The function of this exercise was to stand in place of a control group; that is it was designed to help to establish whether or not the observed outcomes of direct work were solely due to the M.A.R.S. intervention, rather than occurring as a result of some other mechanism. The intention was that statements about the effectiveness of the Project derived from examination of the extent to which internally set objectives had been met would be reinforced by an independent element.

That such reinforcement is needed, and furthermore that ideally it should be provided by a controlled experiment, is a proposition that commands widespread support in certain research traditions, and (perhaps even more so) among lay consumers of research. If a 'special' service is provided as an alternative to a 'normal' service, it is argued, the experimental design is necessary to establish whether the former is more effective than the latter. Thus Jones (1985) in her evaluation of a New York special fostering programme used an experimental design to compare outcomes of those going through the special programme with those receiving a conventional service only. She states firmly that 'without some sort of control or reasonable comparison group, **absolutely no claims** can be made about the success of preventing foster care can be made' (p147, emphasis added). Say that the criterion for success for a particular experimental service is the avoidance of entry to care, and a controlled experiment is conducted:-

1. If a proportion of cases in the control group avoids care, then one would assume that a similar proportion of cases in the experimental group would likewise have avoided care without the experimental service. This proportion must in some sense be deducted from an effectiveness rating for the service based purely on the numbers avoiding care in the experimental group.

2. If a high proportion of cases in the experimental group enters care despite the provision of the service, this may reflect good targeting, i.e. the cases most at risk have been taken, a proportion of whom would be likely to fail whatever intervention was offered. Without a control group, whose failure rate may be compared, there is no way of knowing what allowance must be made for this.

3. The size of the disparity in outcome between the two groups is the measure of the effectiveness of the experimental service, assuming of course that it is in the right direction. (Note, however, that there is scientific no way of estimating, once statistical significance has been reached, how large this disparity has to be before the experimental service can be seen as successful. This is a matter of policy judgment.)

The power of these principles must be acknowledged, but for several reasons a control or comparison group was difficult to set up in the M.A.R.S. study. In the first place, random allocation of cases to M.A.R.S. and to conventional social work was so unlikely, given ethical considerations and the independent referral procedures of the Project, that it was swiftly ruled out.

The alternative of constructing a control group of cases matched to those

70

referred to the Project was considered. However, the M.A.R.S. referral criteria specified not only the imminence of crisis or breakdown but also included the strong proviso that referred cases should have exhausted conventional responses in the statutory sector. Cases would therefore have had to be matched not only on personal characteristics and 'problems', but also on features of their previous careers as clients; it was by no means clear which of the many possible career variables would have been relevant, nor that the indicators would have been available from records. This would also have required a larger sample than was feasible.

A third factor was the expectation that the referral or screening process for intake to the Project was apparently designed to catch the highest-risk cases in the catchment area. This seemed inherently unlikely to be achieved, since social work agencies do not work as consistently or 'rationally' as that, but it would nonetheless be the case that the better the targeting the more unlikely it would be that a true control group of similar cases could have been assembled. The attractive strategy of using a waiting list of similar cases was not available as the Project did not seem to be over-subscribed; some cases were screened out at referral, but usually on the grounds of inappropriateness - generally described as not meeting the criterion of conventional possibilities having been exhausted. A further complicating factor was that this screening process did not operate entirely consistently, cases occasionally being accepted for direct work despite not being considered entirely suitable on the grounds that 'damage' was too severe (see Chapter 3).

While some of these considerations relate purely to the present study, others are likely to apply quite widely in social work research. In this case, they combined, fairly typically, to make a controlled experiment a daunting proposition on purely practical grounds. But even if these difficulties could have been overcome, there would have remained the conceptual problems associated with the experimental design (Clarke and Cornish 1972), chiefly those of achieving adequate control of 'treatment' variables. Without a greater degree of researcher control over what is actually provided by way of input to both experimental and control groups than is usually possible, the findings of an experimental study are usually subject to precisely those problems of interpretation that the design is meant to overcome.

Thus, it might have been possible to identify and describe the features of the M.A.R.S. service that purported to distinguish it in general from those of the statutory services; to do so would have required the identification of a hypothesis, on the basis of exploratory work, concerning the critical variable that characterised the Project. This is a legitimate approach, but we have seen enough to realise that M.A.R.S. does not represent a single intervention approach but a combination of time and particular skills and ways of working. It would have been difficult both to operationalise such a compound variable, and to ensure that any control group cases received no such intervention from their statutory workers or from any other source.

The prediction exercise

The prediction exercise was set up to provide an alternative approach to the control group dilemma. More particularly, it was designed to explore the feasibility of a novel approach to answering the question a control group purports to, namely the extent to which what happened to the group of M.A.R.S. cases was attributable to the intervention of the Project, rather than to some other extraneous factors which might have influenced the outcomes. The exercise involved the use of a panel of 'predictors' working with a collection of case histories.

A number of cases was identified who had actually been referred to the Project and whose provisional outcomes were known. The previous histories of these cases up to the point of their referral to M.A.R.S. were concisely summarised, and submitted to the attention of a five predictors familiar with the local child care scene. These were asked to assess the degree of risk in each case, and to predict the likely course of events **if referral to M.A.R.S. had not taken place.** The rationale was that differences (if any) between the predicted outcome, without M.A.R.S.involvement, and the actual outcome, with M.A.R.S. involvement, were hypothesised to be a measure of the impact of the Project's work (and that alone) on the development of the case.

The predictors were chosen to reflect a range of perspectives on the child care system. They consisted of a social work academic, a reporter, a children's panel member, and two experienced departmental social workers, one a member of the child care review team, and one of the out-of-hours team. Predictions were elicited by interview, and the predictors were seen individually, so there was no group effect on their deliberations.

Cases from the Project's books were selected for submission to the panel. To qualify for inclusion, cases had to have outcomes that were known (even if only provisionally), and reasonably clear-cut in order to simplify comparisons. The outcomes were also those regarded as successful. (This is not cheating. The point of the exercise was to establish not simply whether outcomes were successful but that successful outcomes could be ascribed to the intervention of the Project.) Seven recent cases were chosen on these criteria. The case histories appear as

Appendix 1, with the addition in each case of a brief account, not shown to predictors, of the actual outcome. One case was excluded from parts of the analysis because its outcome proved to be more ambiguous than had seemed likely when it was identified; it was the most recent of the cases.

After some deliberation, it was decided that, rather than predictors being simply asked 'what would happen if...?' the prediction process should be structured in some way. Predictors were supplied in advance with the following notes of guidance.

Notes of Guidance for Predictors

Assumptions

1. The time period for prediction should be up to one year.

2. Unless otherwise specified, the social worker should be assumed to be neither above nor below 'average' in experience or skill, in caseload, and in competing priorities.

3. Similar assumptions should be made about the quality and level of supervision.

4. Conditions of working are those which have obtained in Dundee during the last year, with the exception that the M.A.R.S. Project is not an option.

Questions

Basically the question is 'what is most likely to have happened in this case during the next year?' It may help to approach this by structuring your answer around the following more specific questions:

1. What is the child and/or family at risk of in this situation?

2. What kind(s) of intervention would be likely to prevent that?

3. What is the likelihood of that intervention being provided?

4. What would be the likely consequences of its not being provided?

5. Are there any comments you would like to add about this case?

The results, given seven cases and five separate predictions on each, and producing in the analysis a series of complex grids, will be summarised only. A sample grid appears at Appendix 3.

The most significant responses appeared to be those giving the identification of particular types of risk, the likelihood of intervention being provided to forestall the risk, and the consequences of non-provision. If the risk was seen as serious, and required intervention from conventional sources unlikely - and therefore the risk unlikely to be avoided - then the finding would be that the avoidance of the risk in reality was attributable to M.A.R.S. The stringent criterion adopted in the analysis for firm identifications of risk, likelihood and consequence in each case was that four out of the five predictors should agree.

A second point of interest was the question concerning what type of intervention was seen by predictors as that needed to forestall the risk. If predictors' assessment of this corresponded to what was actually offered by the Project, then it would constitute a measure of support for its methods, independently of the prediction itself. If, however, it did not, the interpretation of the predictions becomes uncertain. This ambiguity in the logic of the device arose from the prior decision to provide the pre-structured questions, and was not foreseen. The questions did however seek to make explicit what was judged to be the predictors' most likely chain of reasoning.

First we shall consider the extent of consensus among the predictors; clearly, if there was no consensus the exercise would fail. (In what follows the cases, some of which have already been encountered, are identified by initials.) In six out of seven cases there was either unanimity or 4/5 agreement on the identification of risks. These risks were identified as follows:

DM:	List D/secure unit
JS:	List D/custody
SM:	offending and long-term custody
C:	family disintegration, abuse, entry to care
SP:	inappropriate List D/G
AH:	family crisis, abuse, school refusal, serious behaviour problems

In the seventh case, only three out of five predictors saw the boy as seriously at risk, though one of the others saw a risk of inconsistent handling by professionals; among the three who did detect serious risk, there was disagreement about the nature of that risk. This case was therefore disregarded in further analysis. Overall, however, there seemed to be a reassuring measure of inter-predictor agreement.

In the case of 'intervention needed', the predictors tended to make several alternative suggestions for each case. Because of the range of these, it was more difficult to assess consensus. There was also a problem in that differing levels of inward knowledge of social work among the predictors produced suggestions differing in the level of detail they incorporated into the descriptions. It was decided to take as the determining criterion here the inclusion of one or more of the elements of intervention actually provided by the Project for the case. By this criterion, each of the six cases remaining in the exercise was seen by all predictors as requiring some elements of intervention in common, including at least one from among those actually offered.

On 'likelihood of intervention', the stringent criterion (using 4/5 agreement) produced a consensus in four out of six cases that the required intervention was unlikely in conventional social work. The remaining two cases attracted agreement among three out of five to the same effect. To use these latter two cases to draw conclusions would therefore involve relaxing the stringency of the exercise.

Finally, and perhaps obviously, the consequences of intervention not being provided were seen as one or more of the identified risks coming about.

It will be noted that the degree of consensus decreased as the exercise proceeded. While one would not, of course, expect consensus to be complete, the degree of its absence that would serve to invalidate the exercise is uncertain. One way of avoiding the problem would have been to involve the participants in a group prediction session. This, however, would have incurred the criticism that agreement negotiated in this way might have represented a manipulated consensus. An alternative might have been to carry out a validity check of the kind described towards the end of the chapter.

How, then, are we to interpret the results? It will be remembered that one case was disregarded because he was not agreed by predictors to be seriously at risk, and that a second case (DM) was to be excluded from the final analysis because the actual outcome had become uncertain. This left five cases whose outcome was known and for whom a prediction was available (with varying degrees of certainty) on summation of the results of the exercise.

Using the stringent criterion of agreement by four out of five predictors, the findings are set out in Table 7.1.

Table 7.1
Actual and predicted outcomes (a)

	predicted outcome	actual outcome
JS	List D school or custody following offences	maintained at home, no offences during involvement of M.A.R.S.
SM	offending, long-term custody	maintained at home, no offences during involvement of M.A.R.S.
AH	abuse and family crisis, serious behaviour problems, likely failure of List G placement	family crisis happened, but period in care used constructively to prepare List G placement, which remained intact; improvement in behaviour

Using the less stringent criterion of agreement by three predictors out of five, the findings for the other two cases appear in Table 7.2.

Table 7.2
Actual and predicted outcomes (b)

	predicted outcome	actual outcome
C	disintegration of family, abuse, entry to care	family maintained intact, no abuse, progress made
SP	inappropriate residential care with schooling on premises	home situation maintained, peer relations improved, schooling problems now truancy rather than refusal

If (but see below) the validity of the method is accepted at face value, the findings are that in three cases out of the six legitimately included success was clearly attributable directly to the M.A.R.S. intervention, and in a further two cases was rather less clearly thus attributable. Had these cases not been referred to the Project, the chances of positive outcomes would in the view of the independent predictors have been much reduced.

A substitute for a control group?

The 'if' a few lines above may seem quite a large one. Nevertheless the idea seemed sufficiently intriguing to warrant following through its logic and some of its possibilities.

The exercise involved taking a putative 'experimental' group (the M.A.R.S. cases) and treating it for the purposes of prediction as if it were not subjected to the experimental conditions; i.e. as it own control group in an alternative universe. It thus enabled an experimental-control comparison to be made, and if nothing else had clear advantages of feasibility. It was, for example, possible to achieve perfect matching, there were economies of data-collection time, and the ethical dilemma inherent in withholding services from clients was bypassed. In some respects it had the advantages of the unobtrusive measure (Webb et al, 1966).

In considering the appropriateness of the device, as opposed to its feasibility, it is illuminating to dwell briefly on similarities with a another research technique developed for rather different purposes, the use of vignettes. This method of studying attitudes, and some of its advantages and problems, have been described by Finch (1987). Respondents are given a vignette constructed by the researcher outlining a social situation and asked what their response would be to it. The respondent may be a member of the public, as in Finch's examples from survey research designed to establish public preferences for the scale and nature of assistance that should be given to vulnerable groups. Another example is that of Fox and Dingwall (1985) where the respondents were professionals and the study designed to establish and compare between different groups prevailing definitions of the need for intervention in cases of alleged child abuse. The various options open to those using the method includes the use of real or hypothetical situations, and the building in of dynamic possibilities to probe the finer points of respondents' attitudes, so that details of the vignette may be progressively altered or supplemented to establish more firmly the triggering points for particular responses.

Although (unlike in our case) the responses here are themselves the subject of the study, or dependent variables, there are points of comparison. In both cases respondents are asked to respond to scenarios selected or constructed to show a concrete human situation. For Finch, this way of testing attitudes which is grounded in complex reality represents one of the advantages of the vignette. A criticism of the experimental model is that it consciously avoids multi-variate situation by seeking to exclude all that is considered (sometimes ruthlessly) 'noise'. The closer the control that is exercised over experimental and control conditions, the more clearly do findings emerge. Yet it is precisely this degree of control that belongs to the laboratory rather than the field: the risk is that the better the experiment, the less realistic the conclusions. As Smith (1975) remarks in his discussion of yet another technique (simulation exercises)

> ... understanding complex social phenomena requires examining complex systems of interaction rather than isolated entities, multivariate rather than univariate analysis, and dynamic rather than static phenomena. (p256)

These arguments highlight the ways in which the use of scenarios enables the inclusion in the analysis of elements of 'dynamism' and 'complexity'. How do these points relate to the context of the present study?

A comparison with the experimental study of Jones (1985) referred to earlier is instructive. Jones's study, really a quasi-experiment since despite random allocation there was little control over comparison group conditions, compared outcomes on the single criterion of entry to foster care; it was obliged to assume, even though the author clearly knows better, that this is a single and unchanging entity whose meaning, in terms of 'success' or 'failure', is unproblematic. (There are also questions, acknowledged by her, about lack of data on what happened to the comparison group.) A looser and less reductionist approach to the treatment of outcome, one which allows for non-standardised measures of success, would seem to have advantages of realism, and the capacity of the M.A.R.S. predictors to hold in their minds a complex series of possibilities enabled this to happen. It may be argued, however, that in principle it is perfectly possible for the experimental model to adopt non-standardised outcome measures, especially as in the prediction exercise described they were to some extent standardised post hoc by the researcher. Perhaps here it is a question of numbers: the greater the sample size, the smaller is the possibility of detailed qualitative work of the kind necessary for non-standardised outcome measures.

A more interesting argument from complexity turns on the legitimacy of treating 'special' (experimental) and 'normal' (control) inputs as having common objectives. The classic design seems to assume that both inputs are pursuing the same ends, or at least that they should be treated as though they are. There are circumstances in which this is entirely legitimate, when for example the intention is to test some overarching service objective. This was the case in Jones's study, when the political legitimation of the special programme was to prevent entry to care, whatever other things may have been going on in the service. In the case of the M.A.R.S. study, however, it was clear that the intervention was pursuing its own distinctive and *sui generis* set of objectives.

This point has two kinds of purchase on the argument. In the first place, the actual practices of the Project, in setting its objectives in individual cases, was certainly wider than preventing entry to care, though that was the principal item in its official charter. Thus in some cases entry to care had already happened, in others it was a more remote possibility than the formal referral criteria would imply, in yet others the role of the Project was to manage admission in instances where that had been agreed to be in the child's interests. This broadening of official criteria for referral seems a near-universal phenomenon in social services agencies.

Secondly, and more particularly, a simple comparison between the M.A.R.S. cases and those of, say, conventional social work was rendered problematic because of the very features which made M.A.R.S. a 'special' form of intervention. The fact that the Project was able to pursue work that was significantly more intensive than the statutory workers itself generated a more complex and detailed set of objectives. Some of the latter could be construed as means to the end of avoiding entry to care or breakdown; others, however, seemed rather to assume the status of independent objectives in their own right, derived from normal social worker's adjustment to developments as they came up in the life of a case, but where more time and resources were available than to the statutory workers.

A further dimension is invoked by the 'dynamism' of the work in practice. As has been shown, the intensity of the work and its duration in some instances produced a tendency for objectives in individual cases to change over time, sometimes in quite radical ways, as either circumstances changed or the workers' understanding of the case underwent significant development.

If the complexity and dynamism of the work empirically undertaken by the Project is set against its stated objectives, which (according to the textbooks) should form the basis for evaluative study, there are several possible responses. On the one hand, one might say that although M.A.R.S. workers were pursuing objectives that were less narrowly defined, this should be irrelevant to the exercise of evaluating their achievement in avoiding entry to care. On the other hand, one could argue that to treat them as having similar goals to those of a less intensive form of intervention would be to denature and trivialise the activity being studied. Whether evaluative study should focus relatively narrowly on a major objective, or whether it should embrace more comprehensively the full range of an agency's activities is no doubt a decision which needs to be taken in the context of individual studies. If the holistic approach is taken, there is a risk that like will not be compared with like in an experimental design which contrasts the 'normal' with the 'special' service. Indeed, the special service can then only be evaluated, somehow, from within, on its own terms.

If, then, the prediction approach can overcome feasibility problems, and if there are some grounds for thinking that in reproducing the complexity and dynamism of the phenomena under investigation it has some advantages of appropriateness over the classic experimental design, how does it fare in the fundamental questions of reliability and validity?

The issues here concern both the basic material and the deliberations of the predictors: the content of the case histories; whether predictors make similar predictions to each other; whether a different group of predictors would have made similar predictions; the validity of the predictions themselves. In the exercise as carried out, where there were partial answers only to these questions, a number of alternative options were open about how to tackle the exercise.

On the first issue, the histories were assembled using primarily M.A.R.S. material, supplemented by information from interviews with referrers, sources of information whose reliability was generally supported throughout the study. They were found to be usable by the predictors. It seems reasonable to conclude that the basic material was a reasonable reflection of the information available to those involved in making decisions.

The second and third issues are ones of inter-predictor reliability. This is perhaps sufficiently dealt with by the note taken in the analysis of the extent of consensus. It will be remembered that lack of consensus at differing stages of the process was taken as a reason for excluding cases from the analysis. The precise procedures used, however, may be felt to cut both ways. It was possible to establish a measure of reliability by structuring the prediction by means of a series of specific questions. Another possibility considered, that of simply asking 'what would have happened if...', would have left open the possibility that the predictors meant different things by similar answers; as it was, the fact that the series of questions was cumulative more or less ensured that the degree of consensus declined as the exercise proceeded. As a result, the conclusions could only be drawn by weakening the more stringent pre-set condition of consensus. A second alternative, carrying out the exercise on a group rather than an individual basis, has the pros and cons described earlier. In passing, it might be noted that the extent of consensus actually found on the first question asked had the unanticipated function of confirming some other parts of the data, such as the success of targeting cases of agreed risk.

The issue of the choice of predictors is a more thorny one. As stated, they were chosen to represent different service perspectives, but to share local knowledge (although in the event the latter was not achieved with complete success). It would have been equally possible to select individuals from the same perspective, and/or those without local knowledge. Would either of these choices have made a relevant difference? The decisions actually made can be plausibly defended, the first for the avoidance of single-perspective bias, the second in the interests of a more realistically grounded set of predictions. Each, however, could be argued the other way. The risk, not altogether avoided, of differing baseline perspectives on social work carrying with them differing views on the likely outcomes and differing criteria for judgement as to how they are arrived at might weaken the findings somewhat. The advantages of local knowledge might be offset by the danger that such knowledge would include awareness of the service being studied, and hence of a source of contamination creeping into the exercise. In principle it would be perfectly possible to test these possibilities by repeated trials using different panels of predictors. If differences in patterns of predictions between groups were found, a judgement would still be necessary as to the most 'valid' choice, or, indeed, as to whether this would invalidate the exercise altogether.

The major issue, however, is that of the validity of the predictions themselves. Can the predictors really arrive at a set of predictions which carry conviction and therefore assume the status of evidence? The predictors themselves had no difficulty in taking the exercise seriously, and many of the incidental observations they made were, in the light of the researcher's privileged knowledge of the cases, extremely acute. The experience of actually carrying out the exercise generated a certain amount of confidence in its face validity, though this will cut little ice with sceptics and as has been stressed there are many uncertainties in the chain of inferences involved in drawing conclusions.

In principle, again, there are a number of ways in which the exercise could have been subjected to more rigorous scientific tests of its validity. Repeated trials could have been made of the nature and levels of information provided in the case histories, to check on the possibility of responses being determined by the way information was presented - an especially sensitive issue in that the prime source of information was the Project itself, whose own habits of structuring case narratives might be thought to have had relevant effects on the way they were read by others.

The most intriguing possibility, however, would have been to build into the exercise its own comparison group by including among the cases a number which were not referred to the Project (and who therefore would have received conventional social work services only) and whose outcome was known. This would permit an estimate of the expected degree of error in the prediction process, and hence enable allowances to be made in drawing conclusions. It would be important to include a mixture of different outcomes. The most damaging result of such a trial would be for negative outcomes to be consistently predicted for cases which had positive outcomes, and if this were found the approach would immediately be consigned to the dustbin of failed ideas. More problematic would be a finding of mixed success in the accuracy of the predictions. It would be a matter of judgement as how far short of perfect accuracy the score would have to fall before the approach was called into question.

A trial of this kind would have the additional implication that the teasing speculation about the most appropriate group of predictors would be redundant. It would simply be a matter of selecting the most accurate, though who that turned out to be in any given context would be an issue of some interest in its own right. The debate about the structuring of the interview would also assume less importance if the criterion was accuracy - with hindsight the course adopted in the exercise may be seen as a distraction consequent upon anxiety about the accuracy of the predictions and the difficulty of the predictors' task.

If too allowance has to be made for, say, a 75 per cent accuracy rating for the predictions, further implications also arise for the numbers of cases in the exercise. As described, it could clearly be carried out realistically with a small number only. Since the study sample was in any case small and this aspect of it was exploratory, it was appropriate to use a lengthy interview to elicit predictions. Given careful advance preparation, however, there is no reason in principle why this could not have been done by means of a self-completed questionnaire, nor why this should not be partially or fully pre-coded to simplify analysis, thus allowing more cases to be included. This would involve the familiar trade-off between numbers and subtlety of outcome measures, but the dilemma occurs in many other approaches.

Finally, a further issue that is equally not confined to the prediction approach is the treatment of time. As noted, it was decided to ask the predictors to consider one year as the period during which their predictions were to apply. This worked satisfactorily enough as a rule of thumb, but participants found it hard to stick to literally. As also noted, the actual outcomes might have looked different (whether more or less favourable) if a longer period had been used. It is a fact of social work research life that some types intervention, with some individuals, take longer to bear fruit than others, whereas research studies need to be time-limited. This is a question where arbitrary judgements are inescapable.

There are obvious difficulties in the conception and interpretation of the prediction approach, and the present writer is undecided about the value of pursuing the considerable battery of testing rituals which would be needed to establish more firmly its reliability and validity. There are also considerable difficulties, however, in more traditional approaches. The use of judgements made by 'experts' is not unknown, and social work researchers are likely to have frequent recourse to methodological devices of uncertain scientific standing.

In the next chapter we return to somewhat more conventional ground in reviewing evidence for the impact of M.A.R.S. on the statutory agencies.

8 M.A.R.S. and the social work department: Influencing the practitioners?

We have seen some of the problems and possibilities in assessing the effectiveness of the Project's direct work with clients. The difficulties in exploring the ancillary aims of M.A.R.S. - that of making an impact on the working of the statutory agencies - and in investigating other aspects of its relationship to those agencies were just as great. In principle, there could be various kinds of 'impact': on skills, techniques, planning, attitudes to and ways of thinking about clients and their problems, about the use of resources, about inter-agency working, and so on. In none of these areas are indicators of impact easy to come by, but it was necessary to give some attention to them, since they were clearly an important part of the M.A.R.S. enterprise. At the same time, conversations with social workers suggested very quickly that there were additional issues about the relationship of M.A.R.S. to the statutory sector that might significantly affect any assessment of the overall effectiveness of the Project.

One relatively hard fact pertinent to the potential impact of the Project on social workers was the number of the latter in contact with M.A.R.S. during the study period. Counting basic grade workers only, and including the various kinds of consultancy as well as the direct work contact, this came to twenty over a six-month period. (Interestingly, this was reported to have increased significantly subsequent to the completion of the study.) Several of these made more than one referral to the Project, and two workers each had three of their cases among the sample of twelve.

This chapter reports the perceptions held of M.A.R.S. in the statutory sector, primarily in the social work department. As well as material from interviews with the seven field social workers carried out in relation to the direct work cases, the discussion draws on interviews with the senior social workers (team managers) in the five area teams which fell within the Project's catchment area and which had responsibility for children and adolescents. Two area managers, the hospital social work manager, and the head of the assessment and review team were also interviewed. Although there are obvious problems in trying to assess impact on the basis of how individuals say they have been affected, the views they expressed will be reported for the light they shed on this. But there is perhaps a prior question of how M.A.R.S. is seen in various respects by its principal referring agency, which is difficult to separate from the question of impact.

The concentration will be on the senior social workers (SSWs), who were interviewed on the assumption, which proved well-founded, that they would have an overview of a number of referrals to M.A.R.S. over a period of time. (It will be remembered that the Project tried to insist on the presence of SSWs at the crucial referral and feedback meetings.) They were asked about referral criteria and processes, the M.A.R.S. style of working, its impact in general on both clients and social work practice, and the overall strengths, weaknesses and effectiveness of the Project. Material from interviews with area managers and from those basic grade workers with individual cases is also used. In the interests of preserving respondents' anonymity, it will not necessarily be made clear to which category a respondent belongs.

The M.A.R.S. perspective on social work

First, however, it is helpful to set the scene by looking back on the M.A.R.S. perspective on statutory social work. We have noted (Chapter 3) that Project staff had particular images of statutory work and on the type of referrals received from the department - almost amounting to a 'M.A.R.S. culture'. Social workers were said to be inhibited by workload and bureaucratic conditions of working. It was thought important for M.A.R.S. to avoid taking over complete responsibility for a case, in order to maintain social worker involvement and 'leave some skills with them'. There was thought to be an increasing tendency for referrals to be of 'kids in limbo', placement breakdowns for whom appropriate resources were unavailable. Some of these components of the M.A.R.S. culture will be seen to have their mirror images in the perspective of social workers on

M.A.R.S.

There was further elaboration of some aspects of the M.A.R.S. culture. The method of influencing social work practice was seen as being almost exclusively through personal contact over individual cases. If it was a question of seeking to change certain practices, then the means would be through people rather than through systems, and primarily through the working example of the Project's approach to cases. The position of the social worker engaged on a case with M.A.R.S. was recognised as being a difficult one:

> We're actually putting the social worker in two cultures, we're putting them in our culture ... and they're going back to their own team who don't understand, who don't sympathise with what we do ... we're creating quite a lot of tension for them.

A further source of 'tension' for the social workers was said to be the apparent contradiction of their retaining case accountability while a high proportion of client contact was in the hands of the M.A.R.S. worker:

> They [social workers] have to trust us entirely if it's a risk family, but **they're** ultimately going to be on the carpet...

It seemed important to compare these definitions of their situation by the M.A.R.S. staff with those of departmental workers.

The social work perspective on M.A.R.S.

The perspective in the social work department was not monolithic; just as M.A.R.S. had developed a team culture, it would be reasonable to assume that area teams had also, especially as these were specialist teams. What is being examined here is likely to be the result of particular histories within teams of encounters with the Project, including those dating from an earlier period with different M.A.R.S. personnel. While there were significant common themes in the interviews, there were also, therefore, significant disparities of view. In reporting them, an attempt is made to do justice to the spread of views, without undue weight being attached to any one unless it was particularly widespread.

Referral criteria

The existence of the memo setting out formal referral criteria (see Chapter

2) was widely known, its contents less so. Those aware of the criteria treated them with some scepticism, suggesting that the stipulation of, for example, imminent reception into care was outdated both by declining use of residential care and by the fact that the Project was known to take a wider range of cases. Most commonly, the idea of there being 'a typical case' for referral to the Project was denied, and some respondents were concerned to take a more knowing and realistic view of the purely contingent ways in which social workers made use of extra-departmental resources. This was seen to depend, for example, on how well they knew the individuals and on how much trouble needed to be gone to for the resource to be obtained. Typifications of what might be a particularly appropriate situation did, however, include: school breakdown, with a need for individual support in an educational package; specific and time-consuming work with the client (such as counselling) where the social worker had other commitments in the case; the need for a speedy assessment, or for one of a thoroughness to which the social worker had no time to commit. Some resentment was expressed at an impression said sometimes to be given by M.A.R.S. of being a 'last ditch' agency, to be called upon when all other efforts had failed: this was thought to provoke resistance among the statutory workers to making a referral.

Referral processes

There were two main themes here. First, the referral processes were said to be threatening to social workers, who often felt deskilled, even 'in awe' of the Project, especially if they were themselves inexperienced. This was linked in respondents' minds to the intensity of referral and feedback discussions, which itself was linked to the time that M.A.R.S. staff (unlike social workers) were able to devote to them. It was also ascribed by some to the self-presentation of M.A.R.S. staff, though the tendency was to say that this had been more marked in the past. Secondly, however, the same intensity was also seen in a more positive light, as forcing the worker to 'concentrate the mind'. For one respondent the fact that the social worker was in a negotiating position, not having an automatic right to a resource, was important. This could be useful in stimulating a deeper scrutiny of a case, but could also be frustrating. If the latter reaction was evoked, this could operate as a disincentive to making future referrals. The referral stage was also believed, more by social workers than by their seniors, to be a source of learning about techniques, such as interview skills, clarifying objectives, and ensuring that issues were fully confronted at multi-disciplinary case discussions.

A universal comment was to highlight the frequent tendency of the

Project to ask workers to commit more time to a case than was thought realistic.

Style of working

This rather loosely defined topic attracted a variety of responses. The M.A.R.S. way of working, seen through the eyes of the social workers, evoked different and sometimes contradictory reactions. Positively, some again saw the joint planning and shared working as a learning opportunity at the level of technique, as a pattern which encouraged constant re-evaluation of case progress, and as a model of good inter-worker communication. Notably, there were no complaints about the Project failing to share information. The 'stickability' of the M.A.R.S. plans, once formed, was commented on.

There were some negative comments, however, some of them surprising in the light of the Project staff's view of themselves. The Project was seen by some as operating what was variously described as a 'quasi-psychoanalytical approach to assessment' ('they're a bit up on cloud nine at times'); and a 'medical model', featuring the use of pathologising labels to describe parents and being wedded to an 'instrumental' view of social work. In the context the latter view was contrasted by the respondent with the systems approach, with connotations rather different to those implied by the M.A.R.S. workers' own use of the same term (see Chapter 5). For one respondent, the M.A.R.S. style of working was not to tackle family systems and work positively with them, but rather to divide a case into child and family 'segments' with, as often as not, the statutory worker handling the parental dimension. This was portrayed as evidence of the Project tending to take the 'soft option' in doing relatively minor work with children while distancing themselves from the really challenging work with adults, of their reluctance to 'get their hands dirty', and even of their 'desire to be liked'. This respondent, whose strongly and unusually negative view has been reported in detail because of the importance of the issues raised, also felt that M.A.R.S. had a negative view of statutory sector fieldwork, and that this communicated itself.

This warrants some comment. To characterise M.A.R.S. as, for example, adhering to a medical model is hard to reconcile with the statements of Project staff, and their postulated disinclination to get involved in family work could be queried by citing various examples, as has been established earlier in the book. It was also apparently contradicted by other social work respondents who saw the Project as possessing a degree of expertise in family work. The point is not to be glibly disposed of, however. There were signs here of a structural contradiction relating to the division of roles between working with the child and working with the family. It is interesting that the phrase 'soft option' was also used by Project staff themselves to describe their preference for working with the child only, though it was not clear that they would have accepted it as a criticism. Rather, it was where they believed their most worthwhile contribution was made.

The underlying issue is whether it was sensible for cases to be shared in the way that M.A.R.S. preferred. The reasons for this preference have been explained as relating to their aims to influence workers, and to discourage referrals made solely to pass on elsewhere the most difficult work. That the sharing created 'tension' for some social workers was (as we have seen) acknowledged. It certainly seemed odd to some social workers that, given the relative generosity of the M.A.R.S. resources, the Project did not take over cases completely. There may also be an issue about confusion for clients when more than one worker was involved and the relationship between them unclear (though data from the client interviews suggested that clients were well able to distinguish between the respective roles of M.A.R.S. staff and social workers). A case could be made that it indeed would have been sensible for M.A.R.S. to take over case accountability, at least when no statutory orders were in force. It would be strengthened if evidence for a positive impact of the Project on social work practice were somewhat thin (see below). There were, however, arguments against put by some respondents over and above those advanced by Project staff, including the following. The social workers' position inside the statutory framework gave them advantages in terms of contacts on clients' behalf with other statutory agencies (schools, the housing department, DSS, and so on). They also had easier access to resources within the department's control. Overall, this remains a problematic element in the relationship between M.A.R.S. and the social workers, and will be returned to at the end of the chapter.

Impact on clients and workers

Social workers' views on the effectiveness of work with individual clients have already been discussed in Chapter 6. The other respondents commented in general terms and guardedly. One wondered whether M.A.R.S. was sometimes engaged in delaying the inevitable by trying inappropriately to prevent admission to care. Others pointed to the difficulties of evaluating work with clients, and to a lack of impact on adult relationships; examples were mentioned where little difference seemed to have been made by the involvement of the Project. All, however, seemed reluctant to commit themselves to a definite view on how effective

M.A.R.S. was with clients, a response which could be interpreted in various ways ranging from genuine uncertainty to due caution when faced with a researcher who might have been collecting evidence which would prove them wrong!

On the effects of the Project on the working practices of social workers, views were divided. Most respondents acknowledged specific contributions in the form, for example, of new ideas or untried alternatives in both direct and consultancy cases. The question was really directed, however, at evidence of any effects which might have carried over into the general repertoire of the worker, outwith the M.A.R.S. involvement. The response among the SSWs was sceptical. While mention was made of interviewing techniques, the habit of explicitness, and clarifying roles in complex cases, this was on the whole lukewarm, and the majority view was that little or no impact of this kind was discernible. One respondent commented that such a view might well be construed as defensiveness, given that in this persons opinion the attitudes of social workers were notoriously difficult to shift. Respondents' attitude to the question would obviously depend on whether they believed that Project staff had superior skills to communicate (see below).

The basic grade social workers were more forthcoming. Apart from aspects mentioned above and under referral processes, mention was made of analytical thinking about family dynamics, and of putting together multi-disciplinary agreements. That the social workers were more positive seemed to lend credence to a view expressed by more than one respondent: the closer the acquaintance with M.A.R.S. the greater the appreciation of their approach and the fewer suspicions entertained.

Overall effectiveness

This was approached in the interviews by asking about the strengths and weaknesses of the Project. By far the dominating feature of M.A.R.S. to be mentioned was **time**: compared with the statutory workers, the M.A.R.S. staff had time ('acres of it!') in which to develop skills and practise them effectively. A social worker commented 'it makes me sick that I haven't the same amount of time to give to other cases'.

There was a clear divide among respondents, however, in how this was interpreted. For some, it was an asset which was accompanied by specialist skills of a high order, and which gave the Project the capacity to act as a model of good practice within the department. Others, however, did not see the M.A.R.S. workers as having skills superior to those of many of their social work colleagues, who, given equivalent protected time, would have been just as effective, if not more so. Within this group,

90

however, were those who acknowledged the usefulness of the M.A.R.S. skills when referring workers were inexperienced, always provided that the effect was not a demoralising one.

Linked with the asset of time was another structural characteristic, that of independence from the statutory framework. This was seen as conferring several advantages on the Project: greater objectivity in analysing a case; the ability to act as a more effective advocate for clients; a better position in liaison with the education department. A particular slant on this came from a SSW who spoke of the beneficial effects on the morale of M.A.R.S. staff which flowed from their being 'protected from the dirty work' (i.e. being able to reject referrals).

A third positive feature, which was also linked in part with the time enjoyed by Project workers, was their ability to provide each other - and collaborating departmental staff - with an enviable degree of mutual support. This was seen as producing a high level of self-confidence (something which communicated itself to social workers), as sustaining commitment to cases, and as being 'a source of inspiration'.

These features which respondents identified as the strengths of the Project may be seen as deriving entirely or partly from its organisational location, operating as it was as an independent unit on the periphery of a statutory department - hence their description as structural. Non-structural items, such as those based on the Project's particular modes of practice, largely included those already mentioned under other headings, and in general figured less prominently in replies to this set of questions.

Some of the reservations expressed about the M.A.R.S. approach have already been mentioned. The most frequently cited negative feature was the 'unrealistic' expectation on the part of M.A.R.S. of how much time social workers would be able to devote to cases. This, which occurred particularly at the initial negotiating stage, evoked reactions ranging from irritation to a serious doubt about the realism of the whole M.A.R.S. approach.

Other features of the referral process found to be problematic included the demoralising effect previously discussed, and the awkward situation that might arise if the referring social worker had approached the Project with a role for M.A.R.S. already worked out, and found that the M.A.R.S. staff were then arguing for a different strategy. It was thought important in these situations for social workers to be assertive and be able fight their corner, and to resist unrealistic Project demands. One SSW observed that the most effective sharing took place when the social worker was experienced and competent.

This reveals what is perhaps a second structural contradiction. In the view of Project staff, one aspect of the need for M.A.R.S. was the high proportion in the area of inexperienced social workers who needed the kind of specialist service they saw themselves as providing. Yet there seems some logic in the view that inexperienced workers are those **least** well equipped for the demands of shared working. On this basis it might have been fruitful to explore the possibility of developing more than one pattern of collaboration between M.A.R.S. and the statutory workers, according to the experience level of the latter. (Data were not collected on the experience of referrers, but an impression was that a majority of those with cases in the sample had several years' experience, and rather more than those with consultancy cases.)

Finally, points were made about the 'image' of the Project. This was seen as a negative feature if the impression had been created that M.A.R.S. 'gave itself airs', believed itself superior in terms of expertise. This was usually said to belong to an earlier stage of the Project's history, but lingering in the minds of some. Alternatively, lack of clarity or understanding of the Project's role on the part of colleagues was an issue for some respondents.

Understanding and impact

It is not easy to summarise such a complex set of reactions to the Project. While there was a fair measure of agreement on what were the most salient of the Project's characteristics, there was also some disagreement; at the same time features of the Project's ways of working which some viewed in a positive light were seen negatively by others. If we attempt to sum up the picture, the features which were viewed **positively** included:

* skills and techniques seen as setting a good example:
  - interviewing techniques
  - clarifying objectives
  - clarifying inter-agency roles
  - inter-agency planning, joint working

* time

* source of new ideas

* assessment process 'concentrates the mind'

* expertise in family work

* independence, objectivity

* readiness to confront difficulties

* 'team spirit' and self-confidence

Negative features identified by some included:

* unrealistic time expectations

* 'airs of superiority'

* referral process threatening or demoralising

* operates inappropriate model (medical, psycho-analytical)

* goes for soft options (children rather than parents)

* should take over case as a whole

There were therefore some examples of the kind of relationship and the kind of influence on workers that the Project would regard as appropriate - perhaps less unanimously identified than they would ideally hope. At the same time there were conflicting attitudes among the social work respondents. There were also indications of various kinds of mismatch between how the Project would like to have been seen by actual or potential referrers and how it really was seen. In so far as there was a lack of fit, it was to be found in the definition of the Project's role, in the nature of its contribution to practice, and in the targets of its intervention. The mismatch seemed most prominent at these broader levels. As we have seen in an earlier chapter, when perspectives on individual cases were examined, there was evidence of a large measure of agreement between Project staff and social workers.

It has, of course, become commonplace (certainly since Smith and Cantley (1984) drew attention to the phenomenon) for researchers to discover that different parties to an episode of social intervention have differing views as to its objectives and impact. And similar problems of communication, conflicting perspectives and 'interface' issues have been particularly noted in relationships between area teams and 'special' units, whether the latter are located within the statutory department or outside it.

One respondent asked, rhetorically, 'are they a service to the clients or to us?' Though it was not clear what the right answer would have been for him, the M.A.R.S. reply would have been 'both'. The main focus of the data collected for this chapter was intended to be on the question of whether M.A.R.S. was able to exert an influence on patterns of practice, as perceived by social work staff. Within the limits of the difficulty of assessing such an influence, the answer is partially positive. But the focus is significantly blurred by the complexities of the interface between a statutory department and a voluntary agency. There is a relatively clear identification both of some positive possibilities of this type of arrangement, and of some problems that are probably inherent in it. The working conditions associated with the status of M.A.R.S. as an independent agency with control over its caseload were seen by social workers as its chief advantage, but also as the source of some of the problems of shared working.

Some of these problems relate to attitudes. It is hard to deny that a mild strain of resentment was to be found in many of the responses of the social work staff, a sense that the situation contained the potential for odious comparisons to be made between themselves and M.A.R.S. This sense, where it existed, was likely to have been exacerbated by any feeling that M.A.R.S. enjoyed high esteem from senior departmental management, as was presumable indicated to rank and file staff by the financial support given to the Project by the department. Another factor could have been a reaction to the material benefits apparently available to M.A.R.S. clients (such as meals in restaurants, outings, holidays), when a social worker might have to go to great lengths to obtain anything resembling these for other clients. While such attitudes might seem unprofessional, a sense of 'them and us' develops in most team or unit cultures, and was also to be found within the Project.

Much of this, as we have seen, focused on the issue of 'time', particularly in the view that the Project made unreasonable demands on the social workers' time when contracts were being negotiated. Social workers might concede that the commitment of time being sought was justified on principles of good practice for that particular case; in the context of their total caseload, however, they might see a referral to M.A.R.S. as a means of freeing them to give time to other work of high priority. Indeed, this might well have seemed to them a rational time-management decision: hence the desire reported for M.A.R.S. to take over cases completely. They may also have been influenced by the thought that they were bound to appear in a disadvantageous light to clients if unrealistic joint undertakings were given and commitments not subsequently met.

Through the eyes of M.A.R.S. staff, who believed that they were well aware of the competing priorities of statutory staff, 'unreasonable demands' appeared rather, in the first place, as a justified attempt to argue for the needs of individual cases to be met. That they were also justified by the Project on the additional grounds that they fell within their aim of influencing departmental practice must be set against the uncertain evidence presented here about the degree to which influence was achievable or seen by the social workers as appropriate.

9 Conclusion

The study reported in this book addressed the problem of clarifying the meaning of preventive work and the means whereby it may be studied evaluatively. Its ambitions can be summarised in a series of questions. When social workers see themselves as working preventively with children and families, what are they seeking to prevent? How can it be demonstrated that 'prevention' has taken place? And, given the largely rhetorical manner in which the preventive role of social work is often discussed, how realistic in practice is the preventive aspiration?

Conceptually the need for clarification of the concept of preventive work seemed acute. It was suggested earlier that most social work activities could probably be described as trying to prevent something, even if this is 'only' the further deterioration of a problem already serious. Yet if the term can be used to describe everything, then it ceases to be a useful way of distinguishing one form of intervention from another. One attempt to increase the purchase of the concept has been to construct models of preventive work which seek to differentiate stages of prevention, for example by using the health-derived terminology of the primary, the secondary and the tertiary. While these terms are helpful at a conceptual level, they are not necessarily productive when it comes to designing a piece of research and isolating a unit of analysis. The reasons for this are interesting for anyone concerned to conduct research in ways that are realistic about and do justice to the complexities of social work practice and its clientele. Clients and their circumstances in the world of practice simply do not fit the typology: their problems, and involvements with welfare agencies, are inextricably linked in a bewildering array of different patterns and processes, and any sustained involvement with agencies generally produces a constantly changing picture.

Such, at least, was the initial suspicion, which prompted the way the study was tackled. Rather than set out a theoretical model and try to use it to categorise and study specific models of preventive practice, it was decided to start instead from what social workers who claim to work preventively actually do. In order to do this, it was probably essential that the example of preventive practice selected for study was characterised by clear and realistic thinking about the 'ends and means' pursued. *Prima facie* the M.A.R.S. Project met this requirement, and the initial impression was confirmed by the experience of carrying out the study. Without a staff group who were systematic and articulate in their thinking about the tasks they undertook, the collaborative exercise of developing a set of preventive goals which reflected the bulk of the Project's work less well. It had been the hope that the categorisation developed here of preventive goals would be capable of application in other contexts. With some modification, the categories have been further explored in the statutory sector (Brown, 1989) and usefully applied in an evaluative study of a specialist area team (Coyle, 1988).

The research on M.A.R.S. was offered in Chapter 1 as a case-study - a term often misused in social policy research. To be of value the case that is studied needs to be selected for some reason other than opportunism. The M.A.R.S. Project was chosen because it was an apparently interesting example of preventive work, and its methods lent themselves to research in the way described above. To locate it more precisely in a wider class of preventive social work agencies, the typologies suggested by Holman (1988), in the UK, and Jones (1985), writing about the American scene, are helpful.

Holman's categorisation distinguishes, by both substance and style of working, the 'client-focused', 'neighbourhood', and 'community development' models. Client-focused centres offer specialised activities, take referrals from statutory agencies, do not have open-door access, and operate on a basis of professionalism rather than (user) participation. Neighbourhood centres provide a broad range of activities, have open-door access and neighbourhood identification, and stress local participation and flexible staff roles. Community development centres do not provide services, are unwilling to take referrals, and stress collective action and local management. In Jones's review of research on American preventive programmes, she offered an alternative classification based on the extent and type of services offered: the 'comprehensive social work services' type provided counselling and the full range of social services; the 'counselling and psychotherapy' type provided diagnostic assessment and individual or family work, but not social services; and the 'service planning' type offers service planning and monitoring, but does not provide any services directly. These categories may be further subdivided according to the intensity and duration of their involvement with clients or users.

In neither case is the terminology used to characterise the models necessarily applicable to M.A.R.S. in all its particulars, as the reader may perhaps be in a position to judge. With this caveat, however, the M.A.R.S. Project approximated most to Holman's client-focused model and to Jones's 'counselling and psychotherapy' type, with high intensity and long duration. As such it appears to be a type of agency less often studied in recent years than those operating the neighbourhood or community model, as were most of those investigated by Holman (1988) himself and Gibbons (1990). Partly for this reason the Project's approach may in some ways appear somewhat old-fashioned (though some would argue none the worse for that), with its allegiance, albeit not uncritical, to 'traditional casework', its prudently controlled caseload, and its carefully nurtured sense of professionalism.

Summary of findings

During a period of six months, the M.A.R.S. Project handled a total of 34 cases, including new referrals and those already in contact at the start. Referrers came primarily from the social work department, but also from the education and health services. These 34 cases represented two kinds of involvement for the Project. Rather more than a third were at various stages of a 'contract', receiving intensive direct work, while the remainder were for consultancy, found to be a catch-all category which could range in scope from a single meeting to a period of extended assessment and joint monitoring with social workers for several weeks. Most of the direct cases lasted longer than six months with the Project, the longest being 18 months and continuing.

The staff's theoretical approach was eclectic and a range of techniques was used. During the rather elaborate referral procedures, great stress was laid on gathering and analysing information from all possible sources, identifying any inter-agency problems, clarifying objectives and roles of involved agencies, and securing the commitment of all parties to them. When plans for direct work were made, they might be to a time limit, or, more commonly, open-ended; follow a ready-made pattern according to

98

precedent (as frequently in the case of education packages), or be worked out from scratch to suit a particular case; be directed at long-term or provisional objectives; be focused on institutional objectives (avoiding care) or personal functioning. Objectives were regularly reviewed and often modified during the life of a case.

A majority of the clients were boys, and the commonest age-group was the mid-teens, though there was a significant minority of younger children and cases where a family as a whole was 'the client'. In accounts given of the problems of referred cases, the formally stated referral criteria were only partially reflected. Although the cases taken by the Project were generally of high risk, the risks covered a wider range of adversity than imminent breakdown. The key to the distinguishing characteristics of M.A.R.S. cases was more likely to lie in the intervention circumstances at the time of referral: when the statutory worker was unable to form a plan because of case complexity, when the need identified was for work too time-consuming for the statutory sector, when there was inter- or intra-agency confusion or disagreement.

When preventive objectives were scrutinised in the direct work sample, a positive picture emerges of the Project's work. Variously calculated, there was a success rate of about 75 per cent in the achievement of objectives, with a notable degree of agreement between Project staff, statutory workers, and those clients who agreed to an interview. The data tentatively suggested a tendency for what was categorised as work directed at the improvement of parenting capacities to be less successful than work directed at the care system, at inter-professional problems, or at children's behaviour.

A more mixed account emerged of the secondary aspiration of the Project to influence wider practice in the statutory agencies. Numerous examples of positive influence were cited, but the focus was blurred by differing views within the social work department of the Project's role and the nature of its expertise. On the whole, those who had most contact with the Project were more favourably disposed towards it. However this may be interpreted, it was clear that the distinctive functioning of M.A.R.S. was related to its structural location and the consequences that flowed from this: the time that was available to devote to casework, the freedom to control its caseload, and the absence of bureaucratic or statutory sector constraints. This was also, however, a source of some problems the Project faced in relating to the main referring agency - and vice versa. This would seem to confirm the clear potential of a voluntary sector agency working in partnership with a local authority department while at the same time pointing up some issues to beware of.

Social work as prevention

The study was undertaken in order to investigate an example of preventive work, even if not one of the early preventive kind where problems are somehow 'nipped in the bud' before they become serious. Such, at least, was the implication of the M.A.R.S. referral criteria as formally stated, though there were in fact problems identified among the sample which were at a relatively early stage in their development. The study should also be seen as examining the extent to which a version of rather traditional, casework-oriented social work was able in spite of a pessimistic climate to make an effective contribution towards resolving the problems of exceptionally 'difficult' children and families. Can wider lessons be learnt from this?

How useful it is to describe the Project as engaged in preventive work is, perhaps, in the eye of the beholder. The attempt to devise a categorisation of preventive objectives was certainly a useful way of describing the M.A.R.S. caseload, and of clarifying the work being undertaken and its aims. In the light of the results of that exercise, the formal referral criteria appeared to be a simplification of what the Project was actually doing. The cases as categorised confirmed the range of disparate objectives being addressed, and, importantly, the different levels of prevention that may coexist in the same case. The most straightforward preventive category, preventing entry to care, did figure in the analysis, but not significantly more often than other kinds of objective, and the Project was really engaged in a broader and less easily definable range of tasks than its publicly stated aims. In view of the mingling of problems within a case, often hidden by both researchers and practitioners when they are obliged to categorise cases on a single dimension, it did not seem convincing to interpret this broader range as an example of the Project departing from its remit or accepting inappropriate referrals.

It might be thought that this refinement of the scope of preventively intended intervention adds realism to the concept of prevention, at the cost of rendering it somewhat more complicated than the models reviewed would promise. It should be apparent from the case material in this book that no-one should be satisfied with a single measure of 'outcome' in cases like these - which term, in view of the fluidity and diversity of what took place in each case, seems to need its inverted commas. The occasional use in the account of the term 'provisional outcome' only partially meets the point. There were some cases in the sample where a specific event of a clearly undesirable nature had been avoided; others where it had, perhaps, been postponed for an indeterminate period; others where it had come about, but in circumstances where a more effective degree of case management had been permitted; yet others where the intervention was less related to avoiding specific events than to enable children or families to survive for a time persistently adverse family or personal circumstances. There were cases where all of these were going on at the same time on different fronts. And finally there were cases where providing a good time for an afternoon, for children whose lives were otherwise bleak, seemed to the author at least to be a perfectly legitimate aim.

It could no doubt be argued that M.A.R.S. was operating in the territory of secondary and tertiary prevention (and perhaps in Hardiker et al's (1991) quaternary area). It seems more realistic to suggest that no particular model of preventive work was being pursued. When goals are specific and geared to a particular event, it is reasonable to assume an intervention pattern which has, as it were, a beginning, a middle and an end, at some point beyond which one may legitimately seek an outcome measure. This was the case in some areas of the Project's work. There was also in evidence, however, an alternative, 'maintenance' pattern, where attempts were made to sustain and help clients through a mass of potentially damaging circumstances in a much less easily definable sequence of intervention episodes, and where no final resolution of overwhelming difficulties was seriously entertained.

Two conclusions might be drawn from this. The first is the perhaps disappointing one that a realistic treatment of preventive practice damages the cutting edge of the concept; when examined in the way described in the study, it seems to dissolve fairly readily into 'thoughtful, caring, good-quality social work'. Against this it could be argued that it remains important to elucidate what kinds of undesirable outcomes social workers can prevent and by what means. The alternative conclusion is that it makes most sense to see preventive aims, or more properly a preventive spirit, as embedded in (good) social work practice than belonging to some special institutional category.

The point of departure for the research was a certain scepticism about the notion of preventive work. This was combined, however, with a sense of concern lest a baby should be thrown out with the bathwater: the baby being the preventive aspirations of social work, and the bathwater being an unsavoury mixture of research technology failing to tie down the concept and measure the outcomes, on the one hand, and professional failure of nerve in a hostile climate on the other. Its point of arrival is the unglamorous but necessary proposition, joining with Parker (1980), Hardiker et al (1991) and other commentators, that preventive efforts can and should be relevant to all stages of intervention.

Appendix 1
Prediction exercise:
Case histories

These case-histories were put together from data on actual cases gathered during the study: but structured for use in the prediction exercise described in Chapter 7. The material under the headings of 'Present situation', 'History' and 'Underlying issues' were given to the predictors, as representing the sequence of events up to the referral to M.A.R.S. The sequel in each case, under 'Outcome' has been added in this appendix.

As well as illustrating the prediction exercise, they serve as illustrative case material for the general work of the Project.

1. Donald Mulligan

Current situation

Donald is 14 and has been in care in the West of Scotland nearly all his life; his mother abandoned him when he was one year old, along with three older siblings, after his father had been sentenced to prison. He is the subject of a parental rights resolution. At the moment he is rather precariously resident in a children's home in Dundee, to which he has only recently (three months ago) been moved at very short notice. He is not going to school.

History

Until the age of 10, Donald lived in Quarrier's Homes, moving as he grew older through their different styles of accommodation. He was then fostered for over a year, but during this time in fact lived with several different members of the foster family when care was disrupted owing to a family bereavement. The arrangement ended with Donald truanting, with disputes about domestic routines, and with him running away back to Quarrier's, where he returned to live. After offences were committed, however, Quarrier's insisted on his removal and he was placed in a residential assessment centre in Dundee, and then in a children's home outside Dundee. While here, Donald, now in touch with his natural father, was encouraged by the latter to abscond and was harboured by him for a time. It is believed that Mr Mulligan's motives are primarily mercenary, and contact had only been renewed when Donald was in his teens. Following this episode, Donald was moved to the children's home in Dundee. This was against his wishes - he would have preferred to go to the assessment centre where he had previously been placed; and which, incidentally, is close to his parent's home.

Donald has expressed no sustained wish to live permanently with his father. He has also had some contact with other family members (a sister, and maternal grandparents. He had no knowledge of his family of origin until he returned to Dundee, and was disappointed and shocked to find that their material standards of living were so poor, when he had imagined them to be higher.

At the moment Donald is refusing to attend school, rather than truanting. Previously attendance has been a problem but much less so. He is not a behaviour problem when at school. As a short term measure, a remedial teacher from the school is going informally to the children's home on a 1:1 basis, but only for one hour per day. A firmer 1:1

arrangement has not been finalised.

To some Donald appears manipulative and confrontational, to others relatively biddable, quite articulate, and indeed possessed of some insight. He has made threats to set fire to the home, and has a history of 'acting out' in the company of older brothers and other boys. There is disagreement within the children's home and within the social work department about the nature and seriousness of his problems. Different voices are arguing that the home should hang on to him, though a well-founded 1:1 teaching arrangement is thought to be a prerequisite; and that the home cannot cope. A List D placement has been mentioned.

Underlying issues

The social worker is fairly new to the case, and has not yet formed a plan, having been buffeted by the sudden and dramatic changes in the boy's circumstances. This is compounded by powerfully opposing points of view within his own department, which not only involve the residential staff but also more senior residential and fieldwork managers. The officer in charge seems convinced that Donald should be removed to a List D school, or even to secure accommodation, although not all his staff agree. Conflicting views are expressed by different staff, but also by the same staff when on their own and when in the presence of the OIC. there is confusion within the SWD about who makes decisions about the boy's placement and about what authority the OIC has. There also appears to be an optimistic view about how long it will take Donald to come to terms with the traumas of the past year, and unrealistic standards of behaviour are being set for him in the home. (Suspicions have even been voiced privately that this is a deliberate ploy to make the boy over-react and therefore justify secure accommodation.) While Donald's refusal to go to school is the overt problem, his constant presence in the home is difficult for both staff and himself. The school are willing to cooperate in a formalised teaching plan, but arrangements are hampered continually by the strength of the conflict in the home. The school feels frustrated and dubious. There is a strong sense that events will overtake any planning.

M.A.R.S. response and (provisional) outcome

At the close of study fieldwork, the M.A.R.S. involvement had lasted six months and was continuing. It was of two kinds. First, a series of meetings within the Social Work department (including both area fieldwork and residential managers) and at the school resulted in a clarification of decision-making responsibilities for Donald. A more settled attitude towards his care had developed, with List D school no longer being seriously on the agenda and the children's home having made at least a provisional commitment to 'hang on' to the boy. Negotiations were in hand for a 1:1 school arrangement. Secondly, a M.A.R.S. worker was having weekly sessions with Donald. These sessions, some of which were videoed to facilitate team discussion of the case, were partly devoted to life-history work. This revealed information about disruptions and discontinuities in Donald's early life, the full complexities of which had not been fully appreciated by the professionals currently involved, and which it was felt was highly significant. The sessions were also used to explore with Donald his views about his future, and the role he might legitimately expect to play in decisions being made about him; much of this turned on his relationship with his natural family and his attitude to school. It was believed that his understanding of his situation and his acceptance of the role of professionals has increased, although his behaviour had not really changed, and there were instances of absconding. The placement was being maintained.

2. Jimmy Shaw

Present situation

Jimmy is 14 years old, subject to a 44(1)(a) order. He is the youngest of a large family with a history of schooling problems; he has just returned to live at home with his parents after spending 18 months in a List D school, but has not yet returned to a conventional school four months after the new term has started.

History

Jimmy had been referred to the List D by a children's hearing. He had failed to attend school regularly when already on home supervision on attendance grounds, had been disruptive in class when he had attended, and on one occasion had threatened two younger girls with a knife. He had also committed the offence of taking and driving a tractor from a building site. In addition, he had been an isolated boy who found it hard to relate to peers, and consequently became aggressive. Earlier, both Jimmy and his elderly brothers had spent periods in care on a voluntary and statutory basis. Their parents drink a lot, and the standard of care in the home had been described as very poor. Though overtly caring in their attitude to Jimmy, they themselves are low in self-esteem and can be destructively critical of their son. The social worker found it difficult to engage with Mr and Mrs Shaw, who tend to dismiss crises once they have passed.

The brothers had finished their education in the List D system, and there had been concern that Jimmy would follow the same pattern. There was a history of marital disharmony, but during Jimmy's recent period away things had begun to see more settled at home, especially now that all the older children had left home. In addition, though he was described as 'a disturbed lad' prior to going away, it was believed that his self-image had improved while in the List D. He was therefore recommended for return home.

Underlying issues

However, given the 4-month delay in finding him a school other than the one where he had previously failed, the improvement that has recently been observed is being eroded and he is said to be unable to enter the new school building. As a result of this, there is a risk of deteriorating relationships at home. Difficulties in achieving reintegration had been

106

anticipated, since he had had attendance problems before going to the List D school, and has missed a lot of schooling, and because it is thought he will have great difficulty mixing with his peers. After lengthy negotiations between education and social work to nominate a school for him, a case-conference held at a school outside his catchment area has decided that an element of 1:1 teaching (perhaps off-site) will be required to help him gradually resume normal attendance. There is little credibility between his school and the social worker: the school expects and requires prompt and reliable support for the plan, but the social worker cannot promise to give this and does not see the case as having high priority.

M.A.R.S. response and outcome

The M.A.R.S. involvement with Jimmy lasted 16 months, and was drawing to a close at the end of fieldwork, with Jimmy having reached school-leaving age. The work, directed at getting him back into some kind of contact with mainstream school attendance, went through several phases: described as a series of gradual steps forward in order not to jeopardise small advances. The school, which had had positive previous experience with M.A.R.S., was supportive throughout. After an initial period of support to 1:1 teaching on the M.A.R.S. premises, a first attempt to transfer the 1:1 sessions to the school was unsuccessful, with the social worker being unable to provide support. When the M.A.R.S. worker began physically to accompany him to school, his attendance improved dramatically. It had been discovered during the support sessions that Jimmy had aptitudes for working with computers, and this was used to integrate him into small group sessions in the school, and (with only partial success) to broaden the sessions to include an element of social education. Although full attendance was never achieved, and Jimmy's ability to mix with peers remained doubtful, he never re-offended, his home placement was maintained, and the collaboration with the social worker (who was working with the parents) developed into what both parties believed to be a fruitful sharing of case responsibility.

3. Sammy Murdoch

Present situation

Sammy is 15, and has recently left the assessment centre to live with his mother, a lone parent. He also spends a lot of time with his maternal grandmother, who looked after him up to the age of five. He has difficulties relating to both of them, and indeed, can be of volatile behaviour towards women generally. Because of Sammy's behaviour, the home placement is thought to be precarious.

History

There has been a long debate about the possibility of Sammy going to a List G school. He has been known to the educational psychologists sincehe was six, when he was identified as not coping in school. He has scarcely ever experienced a normal school, and no-one now believes that integration into a normal school is possible. Sammy is barely literate, though he has reasonable practical abilities. He has spent a period of two years, between the ages of 10 and 12, in a residential special school, to which he was referred more because of his mother's accommodation problems than for the severity of his handicap. He returned home to attend a day special school, from which he has been excluded following unruly behaviour.

He has also committed petty offences, been made the subject of a 44(1)(a) order which is still in force, and spent periods of time in the assessment centre, where has received some 1:1 schooling on the premises. He is currently receiving 1:1 teaching in a variety of venues, the chief educational objective being to improve his literacy. Sammy regards this as a very difficult experience, and the relationship with his (female) teacher does not always go smoothly. He is also very deficient in social skills, and has little experience of such elementary processes as going shopping; his behaviour in social situations can be very 'young'. He plays with 9-year olds, and has great difficult in the IT group he sometimes attends.

Underlying issues

He has latterly been in the assessment centre for over a year, while there was a dispute between the education and social work departments over the provision of appropriate residential care. Having prepared the boy to leave home, the assessment centre staff found it increasingly difficult to help him see his future, and this caused a deterioration in their relationships with him. He is now regarded as too old for the List G placement that has long been canvassed, and so is to return home by default. There is widespread scepticism about how long this will last, and none of the professionals feel that the home placement is where he should be. The social worker's involvement is primarily with Mrs Murdoch, whose life is subject to periodic financial, emotional and health crises.

M.A.R.S. response and outcome

The M.A.R.S. involvement with Sammy lasted seven months, and had ended when he reached school-leaving age during the fieldwork period. It being recognised by all parties that the agency network had been unable to meet Sammy's needs, and that the home placement was very much a second-best, the objective was two-fold: to provide a specific outlet, after his Project-based 1:1 sessions, for the frustration and aggression that often built up during them, and thus decrease the risk of Sammy 'taking these feelings home' with him; and to provide him with experiences that would promote the development of some basic social skills. As the intervention developed, it was also found necessary from time to time for the M.A.R.S. worker to resolve difficult moments during the 1:1 teacher's sessions with Sammy. Sammy was found to have reasonable practical abilities, and the models and household objects that he made with the M.A.R.S. worker gave him 'some credence' at home, where his acting out behaviour, though not markedly reduced, was contained. Some significant progress was also made, in the opportunities provided by outings to buy materials, in his social and practical skills, and he was encouraged to attend an IT group. Through the periodic difficulties, the 1:1 arrangement and the home placement were sustained until his school leaving age was reached.

4. The Chatfields

Present situation

Mrs Chatfield is depressed and experiencing serious problems keeping her family (herself and two children aged 10 and 8) intact.

History

Kim Chatfield (aged 10) was admitted to hospital after drinking bleach while at home. Kim was living at home with her lone-parent mother and 8-year-old brother Arthur. At this point Mrs Chatfield told the hospital social worker that she was having great difficulty controlling Kim. Kim was, she said, frequently carrying out destructive and vindictive acts in the home (destroying ornaments, wetting carpets), and being abusive and defiant when checked. Mrs Chatfield would sometimes hit her and then tell her to go away, as she was afraid that she might hurt the child.

Mrs Chatfield was showing signs of depression. The home was not well managed in a material sense; and in addition she recognised that there was no communication in the family and that she could not get through to her children. Things had got to the point where she was afraid to go out with them because of her lack of control.

It also emerged that there had been a few incidents at school of Kim leaving the premises at lunchtime and taking part in petty shoplifting at the corner shop. There were however no problems of attendance.

The hospital social worker referred the case to the child psychiatrist, who had monthly sessions with the family and with Kim at the hospital, while the social worker visited the family at home when she had the time - this over a period of about a year.

During these sessions, Mrs Chatfield began to include Arthur among her problems, saying that he was beginning to imitate his sister, that he and Kim were 'ganging up' on her and that she could not control either of them. Arthur's behaviour at school was also giving grounds for concern about the future, when he would be a bigger and more threatening boy than at present.

Mr Chatfield had been violent to his wife and to Kim - he had left home some years previously.

Underlying issues

The main problem identified by the psychiatrist was the inappropriate and inconsistent parenting of Mrs Chatfield. She was said to be scared of

110

reprimanding the children for fear of losing them, and to have a flat response to any incident. There was anxiety that Mrs Chatfield was losing her sense of self-worth, and was at risk of 'giving up' on mothering. The psychiatrist felt that the needs of the family were for practical work rather than the hospital sessions, and for some attempt to establish proper boundaries for Mrs Chatfield as parent and for Kim and Arthur as children. However, attempts to arrange for relatives (two sisters and a gran) to assist Mrs Chatfield with mothering tasks had not worked particularly well, and had in fact had a deskilling effect on Mrs Chatfield. The psychiatrist is now concerned that her deteriorating parental capacity will result in the children coming into care.

M.A.R.S. response and outcome

The M.A.R.S. involvement had lasted 17 months by the end of fieldwork and was continuing. It contained several phases, and is an example of the original objectives being superceded by others. At first, the family had regular sessions, in the form of an evening meal, including preparation, eating and clearing up, designed to provide practical help to Mrs Chatfield, through example and direct suggestion, on how to control the children's behaviour, to set boundaries to it and stick to them during the week, and to involve them constructively in domestic tasks. While this over a period of months was progressing successfully, so that the disintegration of the family was no longer felt to be a real possibility and Mrs Chatfield's general morale had improved, highs and lows nonetheless occurred, and a particular domestic crisis over an act of theft by Kim led to an explicit change of role. This new orientation, described as a counselling role, involved a deeper exploration of the family dynamics, in terms of Mrs Chatfield's history of previous relationships, their effect on her self-image, and her identified tendency to scapegoat Kim. Though the mealtime sessions continued, the new objectives were implemented through additional individual sessions with Mrs Chatfield and Kim, and developed a more strictly therapeutic character, with the deeper issues being explicitly sought out rather than avoided. This stage was felt to have been made possible only through the earlier work.

5. Stan Palmer

Present situation

Stan is aged 14 and is in his third year at secondary school. He has not attended school regularly for some time. After a recent period in a residential assessment centre, he has been returned home, subject to a 44(1)(a) order, with a view to restarting school with a 1:1 teaching arrangement linked to the school's integration unit, with some attendance at mainstream classes. This does not appear to be working.

History

Stan was identified from the start of his secondary school career as a loner and a misfit, and during his second year his attendance deteriorated to the point where he was hardly attending at all. Two earlier referrals to hearings for offences (fire-raising) had resulted in no further action being taken, but now he was referred on attendance grounds. The hearing was continued, with the threat of a residential placement if attendance did not improve. It did not, and after the continued hearing Stan was placed in the residential assessment centre.

Stan's school attendance has been a problem since he was aged 6, and he has received remedial education. His three younger siblings, however, are all at primary school with no reported attendance problems.

The parents separated when Stan was 7-8. Both Stan and his mother were victims of violence from Stan's father during this period, resulting, it is said, in a deep alliance between them. At the moment Mrs Palmer is out all day attending a college course. Stan spends his time at home, with no walking the streets and no recent offences reported. There is a theory that his not going to school is somehow a way of hanging on to the relationship with his mother. He claims to be staying at home for fear that the house will be broken into if left unoccupied.

Underlying issues

The plan to restart school via a 1:1 arrangement appeared to work for a time (one month), but attendance afterwards fell away. There is disagreement among the professionals involved about how to proceed. A case conference has discussed the possibility of a List G school, but not all members were agreed. The educational psychologist did not like the school that had been suggested although the social worker agreed with it as an appropriate placement. The second school was suspicious of the

112

educational psychologist, who in his turn thought the school was largely to blame for Stan's problems. The school initially had good relationships with the social worker, though these deteriorated during the case discussions. There is thus a considerable degree of distrust between the professionals which makes the close cooperation that would be involved in devising and implementing another 1:1 package problematic.

The assessment report suggested that Stan found it difficult to cope with peer-group relationships; attempts to involve him in IT have failed. He generally appears depressed, negative and uncommunicative. He is, however, seen by child guidance as bright enough to become frustrated with an unrelieved diet of remedial teaching.

M.A.R.S. response and outcome

The M.A.R.S. involvement with Stan took place before the study fieldwork, and lasted 11 months. It took the form of supporting via individual sessions a 1:1 arrangement based on the M.A.R.S. premises, and working with the social worker towards reintegration into school. After seven to eight months, the personal sessions seemed to have resulted in Stan being less withdrawn and isolated, and more capable of mixing with his peers. An attempt was made to introduce full school attendance, with some M.A.R.S. involvement in ensuring his physical arrival at the school, which was prepared to be flexible. His punctuality, however, was poor, and full attendance was never achieved before he left school some months later - partly, it was believed by M.A.R.S. staff, because the social worker was not able to play a significant supporting role. It was generally believed at the final review at the school that the objectives had been achieved in the sense that a medium-term educational programme had been implemented, and that Stan's personal problems had been worked through to the extent that he was now a straightforward truant rather than a disturbed school refuser. The home placement had been maintained.

6. Alan Hawkins

Present situation

Alan is 12 years old. In the period of just over a year that he has been at his present school, there have been a number of problems over his behaviour, and he has been excluded several times. There had been similar difficulties at his previous school. He has a reputation of being unmanageable, of having a short attention span, and of being very demanding of adults' attention.

History

He lives with his mother and her cohabitee, and their baby (Alan's half-brother). He is, however, in contact with his natural father and frequently stays with him at weekends; this seems usually to be at Alan's initiative. The relationship between Mrs Hawkins and her cohabitee does not appear to be well-established, and there are problems in the household caused by the cohabitee pressuring Mrs Hawkins to choose between himself and her son. In addition, a NAI investigation is currently under way concerning Alan and the cohabitee - otherwise the SWD has not been involved. The cohabitee is not keen for Alan to remain in the home, and the level of tension between them is high, with Alan not being allowed to eat with the rest of the family. There is a suggestion that Alan has been responsible, as a focus for rivalry, for the break-up of previous relationships that Mrs Hawkins has embarked on. In the past the cohabitee has attempted to play a parental role with Alan, but this has been undermined by Mrs Hawkins.

They live in a multi-storey block, and Alan has no effective adult supervision. He is alleged to have committed thefts in the neighbourhood, and has been banned from a local community centre. He is destructive of people's possessions, has no friends of his own age, and is the target of verbal and physical abuse from his peers.

Underlying issues

Alan has been referred to the child psychiatrist, who suspected that there might be a problem with his diet. A special diet has been recommended, but Mrs Hawkins was unable to get Alan to sustain it.

The school sees Alan as being likely to emerge later in his teens as having major problems, of which the first stages only are now apparent. Relationships between the professionals (especially the educational social worker) and the cohabitee are not good, with considerable resistance to intervention.

The school, the educational social worker, and child guidance have gone through the 'special needs' procedure, and a place in a List G school has been agreed, but will not be available for about six months. Meanwhile Alan is receiving small group teaching as part of a specially designed package. His ability to settle in a group situation at the residential placement to which he is unaccustomed is debatable. There is considerable concerned about what might happen at home in the interim, particularly as the mother is pregnant. Alan's half-brother is in a day nursery as the cohabitee would not look after him while his mother worked. With all these factors, there is the possibility of a crisis developing which might distort the plans or prevent adequate preparation of Alan for entry to his placement.

M.A.R.S. response and outcome

The M.A.R.S. involvement with Alan had lasted for 17 months by the end of fieldwork, though it had been reduced to a general monitoring, reassurance and 'keeping in touch' when Alan was on home leave from his List G placement. In the period prior to this placement, a M.A.R.S. worker had individual weekly sessions with Alan as part of his educational package. These were devoted to modifying his unmanageable behaviour with adults, and to widening his social experience through outings and the relationship with an adult. A great deal of reassurance also took place in view of the apparent victimisation of Alan at home. The effect on his behaviour and his morale seemed to be good, with Alan being more relaxed and less demanding in his demeanour outside as well as inside the M.A.R.S. premises. Although shortly before the placement there was a domestic crisis which resulted in a brief period in care, it was not of Alan's making, and the time was able to be used constructively to prepare him for the experience of group living. The List G placement has been sustained and family relationships have shown some improvement.

7. Bruce Russell

Present situation

Bruce is aged 12 years, the youngest of four siblings (of whom the next youngest is 23). He lives with his mother and her cohabitee, and has been on supervision for several years. There is concern because of his mother's alcoholism and because of the unusually close relationship between them, described as 'symbiotic'. Mrs Russell started drinking after the death of Bruce's father, which occurred when Bruce was two. The cohabitee is a very passive man, who has no relationship with Bruce.

History

Bruce has had two periods in residential care, the most recent when at the age of 10-11 he himself asked to go into care. He lived in a children's home for several months, during which time his mother started but failed to complete a course of detoxification. The residential staff described Bruce as wishing to take on adult roles, suggesting that this was what he had done at home, in that he 'parented' his mother and competently used social work jargon. Eventually he ran away from the home to London, where an older brother lived, and returned from there to his own home.

Since this escapade, he has not been attending school; in fact there have always been some problems of attendance. When in school he is not a serious problem, but needs firm handling and preferably an experienced member of staff. In the school's opinion he may end up in a List D school, but they do not yet see that as appropriate. They do not have much faith in the social worker and this is mutual.

Underlying issues

The children's home referred Bruce to the child psychiatrist for an assessment of his relationship with his mother. He was of the opinion that Bruce should not be living at home because the mother has 'little potential', and the relationship would continue to be destructive to the boy. He is however prepared to offer further help.

The plan was that Bruce remain in care, but the social worker has arbitrarily given way to Bruce's demands that he be returned home. The social worker has been seeing Bruce and his mother, both together and separately, and has been trying to increase the mother's confidence and parenting skills. Bruce appears to have a strong sense of loyalty to his mother, but gets fed up with her drinking. More than one of the

116

professionals involved thinks that he is the sort of boy who could be drawn to other children with a propensity for troublesome behaviour. The social worker is uncertain about the strategy she should be adopting, about Bruce's needs and his preferences: to maintain at home or to re-admit to care. Professional fostering has been discussed.

The family has recently moved into a new house. There is concern that this may isolate Bruce further from any support he may have had, so that he is thrown back even more on the maternal relationship.

M.A.R.S. response and outcome

The M.A.R.S. involvement with Bruce lasted one year, and took place before the study fieldwork. It was initially directed at the school problems, and included a behaviour modification approach. He began to attend in a less erratic fashion, but this remained a problem. After some months, however, Bruce asked to be admitted to care and entered the assessment centre on an emergency basis. While there, there were absconding episodes and a suicide attempt. There were now additional elements to the M.A.R.S. input, directed at providing consistency in the way the case was being handled by the professionals involved and in particular at avoiding what was seen by M.A.R.S. staff as collusion with Bruce's tendency to manipulate. After a hearing he was returned to the centre for assessment. The M.A.R.S. contribution to this planning period was to work towards a long-term residential placement in a voluntary sector children's home. This was achieved, and was felt to represent the creation of conditions for a constructive long-term placement, i.e. it was planned and did not signify the abandonment of the problems which a List D school might have constituted. Although recognised as appropriate by the staff of the home, however, the placement subsequently broke down, and Bruce returned to the assessment centre.

Appendix 2
Sample table of predictions

Predictor	Risk for JS	Intervention Needed	Likely in SWD	Consequences
1	non-attendance and delinquency, return to List D, subsequent penal career	achieve normal attendance (co-operation between school and SW); IT focused on peer group r'ships	No No	back to List D with worsened r'ship with parents
2	return to List D with past gains eroded (NB might not be inappropriate)	plan (incl possible voluntary return to List D); school to moderate demands; 1:1; alternative schooling	No No	return to list D in adverse circumstances
3	YOI after more offences	Nothing would help!	N/A	'in the lap of the gods' (should have stayed List D)
4	secure accommodation after more offences	IT; SW to start again and have faith in boy; short term mainstay place; parents to AA	No No possible No	at 'risk'
5	illiteracy, no social skills, family break-down, offences	Intensive SW; IT	No No	school refusal - return to List D

Actual outcome: JS remained at home, committing no further offences; there was a long, gradual, partially successful effort to reinstate into school via 1:1, until school-leaving age.

Bibliography

Billis, D. (1984), *Welfare Bureaucracies*, Heinemann, London.

Bilson, A. and Thorpe, D.H. (1987), *Child Care Careers and their Management*, Social Work Department, Fife Regional Council.

Brown, L. (1989), *Perceptions of Preventive Work held by Social Work Practitioners and their Managers*, Social Work Research Centre Research Report, University of Stirling.

Browne, E. (1978), 'Social Work Activities' in Parsloe, P. and Stevenson, O. (eds) *Social Services Teams: the Practitioner's View*, HMSO, London.

Clarke, R.V.G. and Cornish, D.B. (1972), *The Controlled Trial in Institutional Research*, HMSO, London.

Cheetham, J., Fuller, R., McIvor, G. and Petch, A. (1992), *Evaluating Social Work Effectiveness*, Open University Press, London.

Coyle, D. (1988), *Clarifying Prevention?*, MSc dissertation, The Queen's University, Belfast.

DHSS (1985), *Social Work Decisions in Child Care*, HMSO, London.

England, H. (1986), *Social Work as Art*, Allen and Unwin, London.

Finch, J. (1987), 'The vignette technique in survey research', *Sociology 21*, 1, 105-114.

Fox, S. and Dingwall, R. (1985), 'An exploratory study of variations in social workers' and health visitors' definitions of child maltreatment', *British Journal of Social Work 15*, 5, 467-477.

120

Gibbons, J. with Thorpe, S. and Wilkinson, P. (1990), *Family Support and Prevention: Studies in Local Areas*, HMSO, London.

Giller, H. and Morris, A. (1981), *Care and Discretion*, Burnett Books, London.

Gillham, B. (1980), 'Psychological services and problems of adolescent behaviour', in Upton, G. and Gobell, A. (eds) *Behaviour Problems in the Comprehensive School*, Faculty of Education, University of Cardiff.

Hardiker, P., Exton, K. and Barker, M. (1991), *Policies and Practices in Preventive Child Care*, Avebury, Aldershot.

Holman, R. (1988), *Putting Families First: Prevention and Child Care*, Macmillan, London.

House of Commons (1984), *Second Report from the Social Services Committee - Children in Care* ('the Short Report'), HMSO, London.

Howe, D. (1988), 'A framework for understanding evaluation research in social work', *Research Policy and Planning 5*, 2, 6-12.

Jones, M.A. (1985), *A Second Chance for Families*, Child Welfare League of America, New York.

Millham, S., Bullock, R., Hosie, K. and Haak, M. (1986), *Lost in Care*, Gower, Aldershot.

Packman, J. with Randall, J. and Jacques, N. (1986), *Who Needs Care*, Blackwell, London.

Parker, R.A. (ed) (1980), *Caring for Separated Children*, Macmillan, London.

Rowe, J. and Lambert, L. (1973), *Children Who Wait*, Association of British Adoption Agencies, London.

Rowe, J., Hundleby, M. and Garnett, L. (1989), *Child Care Now*, British Agencies for Adoption and Fostering, London.

Smith, D. (1987), 'The limits of positivism in social work research', *British Journal of Social Work 17*, 401-416.

Smith, G. and Cantley, C. (1984), 'Pluralistic evaluation' in Lishman, J. (ed), *Research Highlights 8: Evaluation*, Jessica Kingsley, London.

Smith, H.W. (1975), *Strategies of Social Research*, Prentice Hall International, London.

Thorpe, D.H., Smith, D., Green, C.H. and Paley, J. (1980), *Out of Care*, Allen and Unwin, London.

Tizard, J. (1973), 'Maladjusted children and the child guidance service', *London Educational Review 2*, 1, 22-37.

Vernon, J. (1986), *True for Us? the Scottish Research Message*, Social Work Services Group, Scottish Office.

Webb, E.J., Campbell, D.T., Schwartz, R.D. and Sechrest, L. (1966), *Unobtrusive Measures*, Rand McNally, Chicago.